MW00622402

CASTING LOVE SPELLS

RITUALS OF LOVE, PASSION, AND ATTRACTION

GREGORY LEE WHITE

Mojo Studio & Conjure Co. Publishing
Nashville, TN

Casting Love Spells
Rituals of Love, Passion, and Attraction
by
Gregory Lee White

Copyright © 2022 Gregory Lee White
gregoryleewhite.com

Text:
Gregory Lee White

Cover Art:
Gregory Lee White

Proofreading:
Gregory Lee White, Roy Hamilton, Virginia Tabor, Carolina Dean

Interior Illustrations:
various artists and illustrators from 1880 to the 1930s

First Edition 2022

Published by
The Mojo Studio and Conjure Co. Publishing
211 Donelson Pike, Suite 111
Nashville, Tn 37214

Printed in the Unites States

ISBN: 978-1737930624

TABLE OF CONTENTS

INTRODUCTION

People seek out love spells when their love is not returned, to get a lover back, or to bring the right love to them. Because face it, we all want to fall in love. Our hearts beat faster when that special person comes around, we want to spend every waking moment with them, and we smile all the time without even realizing it. That initial feeling we get when falling in love catapults us into the heavens and makes the problems of our everyday reality seem less important. But when that love is taken away, and nothing you do can convince the other person that your relationship is worth saving, even the most severe doubters explore spells of magic to make things right again.

This book will explore the art of casting love spells from many different magical traditions, including hoodoo, witchcraft, and other forms of folk magic. But to make these spells work, it is equally important to delve into the dynamics of a loving relationship. Because this is where many people go wrong when performing spells - they light the candles and dress them with oils, they have incense smoldering in the room, and a new moon has just risen. However, if they don't explore the real-world reason that led to their relationship going sour, they are destined to repeat the same mistakes, taking them right back to where the problems began. Because, as cliche as it sounds, love is a two-way street. You can burn all the candles you want, but if you don't take ownership of how you contributed to the relationship going bad, history will repeat itself. There are two sides to every story, and the truth lies somewhere in the middle.

Love magic would mostly be considered a type of attraction magic because it brings you romantic love, a loving partner, or ignites sexual passion. Throughout history, love spells were implemented in several ways: through the written word, using dolls, charms, rituals, or, most famously, by way of mixing a love potion.

DEDICATION

For my husband, Roy. I'm grateful our love
requires no spell to keep it going.

ACKNOWLEDGEMENTS

Much respect and appreciation to Harry Middleton Hyatt,
who, whenever I think I have run out of spells, is there
with his massive 5-volume collection of them to remind
me of just how diverse a spell can be. A big thanks to my
magickal friends who contributed some of their own spells
to this book. I have listed them below:

Adam Darkly
Carolina Dean
Miss Nikki Jean
Reverend Roy
Virginia Tabor
Catherine Yronwode

LOVE MAGIC THROUGHOUT THE AGES

EGYPT AND MESOPOTAMIA

Tablets unearthed in Iraq detail rituals of erotic magic as far back as 2200 BC. An 1800-year-old Egyptian papyrus shows the summoning of spirits in the name of love. A woman named Taromeway petitions the spirits to haunt her love, Kephalas, until he is so overwhelmed with desire for her that he gives in to her need to be with him. Today, this is the equivalent of the 'intranquil spirit' spell where the object of your desire is spiritually tormented until they agree to love you.

Like many other ancient civilizations, Egyptians had a deep belief in magic and witchcraft. Priests would often use spells and blessings to cure illnesses and other physical ailments, but the most powerful magic of all was the love charm. Whether a priest or pauper, all Egyptians wanted to find love in life.

In ancient Egypt, love magic began to evolve as early as the 1st Dynasty. Although evidence is scarce, some scholars have been able to deduce a few details of this practice through hieroglyphic interpretation and archeological excavations. The earliest known use of love spells in Egyptian history was found in mummies dating from the Old Kingdom (2752 – 2181 BC). Through these practices, we gain insight into how love magic developed over time.

The ancient Egyptian word "sr" (seren) describes the feeling of care and affection. It was believed to come from the heart, and that it needed to be expressed through physical contact. As this is described as a 'warm' or fiery type of love, contrasting with "ua" (upegi), which is more like desire or lust, but without any deep sense of care for another person. For example, one of the earliest forms of love spell is on the coffin of Ankh-Mahor who lived during the reigns of Ahmose I and Amenhotep I (1495–1435 BC). It is not clear if his love spell was successful, but this does provide us with insights into how such a spell was used by Egyptians at this time.

Another example of an early love spell used in ancient Egypt is the use of a heart amulet. The heart was believed to be the seat of the soul and also associated with love, so this amulet would have been worn for protection or to attract love. The ancient Egyptians believed that human beings consisted of three parts: body, soul and name. To control someone it was important to have them under control on all three levels. Doing so would assure power and control over their desires, pleasures and even destiny.

ROME & GREECE

In Ancient Rome, love spells were not as ubiquitous as they were in ancient Egypt or in the Bible. It appears that love magic was a more private practice and not something that people wanted others to know. There are few instances of love spells in ancient Rome. One of these is Historiae Adversum Paganos (The History against the Pagans) by Paulus Orosius (395-418 AD). In this work, he describes how a pagan woman cast a spell on the wife of Augustine's friend so that she would abandon their faith.

Philia magic was used by women to keep their male lovers under control and faithful. (Philia, often translated "highest form of love", is one of the four ancient Greek words for love: philia, storge, agape and eros.) The spells often involve female beauty, youthfulness, fidelity in marriage or love, but the strongest common thread is that philia magic turns a woman into an object of desire for men. Philia spells were not about achieving sexual pleasure from men; they were mainly considered medicinal and also provided physical benefits such as preserving one's youthful appearance which kept her beholders captivated with undying admiration.

Bust of Venus, the Goddess of love.

Greeks were also heavily into love spells. Their main goal was to influence the gods' emotions so that they would be more sympathetic and benevolent towards humans in love. The Greeks did this by doing a variety of different things. One thing that a lot of Greeks did for love spells was they would sacrifice an animal or do other rituals to appease the gods. Another major belief was that if people had good intentions then they could influence the gods through these rituals and sacrifices. This is why, throughout history, people have sacrificed animals as well as offered gifts in an effort to influence their relationships with their lovers.

Another common practice in Greece was for men to write songs celebrating the lover's beauty and praise her virtues. For example, while some scholars disagree about the translation, Alcman, a Greek poet from Sparta, composed a hymn to the goddess Athena, called "Partheneion", which praises her as the fairest maiden of all and invites young women to follow her example. Songs can be spells, used to enchant another. The word 'charm' originally meant spell or incantation. These charms were words that were used to bring about change, whether spoken or sung.

MEDIEVAL ENGLAND

During the later medieval period (14th to 17th century), marriage developed into a central institution for public life. This is reflected in their love magic: while the immediate desire was sex, it was most often practiced to secure something more permanent - marriage. So, spells were not just cast upon just anyone in the Renaissance, but on those unions that held special importance. Hiring someone versed in the magical arts was an expensive investment at the time, but the payoff could be greater. Men and women of status were more often the targets of love magic. Economic or social class restrictions would often inhibit a marriage, and love magic was seen as a way to break those barriers, leading to social advancement. These marriages were about money, land, and titles so a lot was at stake. These love spells were meant to be kept secret because, if the victim realized a spell was being cast, there was the chance they may retreat instead of leaning into the magic that was being cast. Secrecy led to the effectiveness of the magic, which is still true today.

During the Renaissance, elements of Christianity seeped into magic rituals. Clay dolls or written spell scrolls were often hidden inside the altar of the church, unbeknownst to the priest. Holy candles, normally used to pray for others, were lit for the purpose of love spells and left out in plain sight. The Host from a Catholic Mass was sometimes taken home and used in magic. To ensure a better chance at success, the caster combined elements of Pagan magic with the power of the Christian church.

The second example of love magic in England comes from William Langland (c.1332-c.1380). In one of his poems, William Langland describes a woman who was in love with another man, but her own husband was a very wealthy merchant. She decided that she wanted her husband dead so that she would be taken care of by the man she loved. To get her way, the woman plotted with another man to kill him, and they succeeded without anyone finding out. In another poem, he talks about one man who falls in love with another woman and leaves him for her husband. This has a major impact on the protagonist, and at one point, he says, "Yowre lay wylt I retorne to me/ Yowre lay wylt retorne to mee." This translates as "Your laughter will return to me."

The 1487 Malleus Maleficarum can best illustrate the view of women within the Renaissance. In the opening section of this text, Heinrich Kramer wrote, "All witchcraft comes from carnal lust, which in women is insatiable." It was a stereotype at the time that only women were practitioners of magic. This dark art wasn't available to men because it called upon the feminine powers, things like menstruation, birth, and fertility - everything associated with a woman's 'shameful parts,' which were a lure for the devil.

Throughout history, people have been trying to influence their love life magically. In ancient Greece, men sang their songs about their beautiful lovers. In medieval England, love magic was curtailed by religion but continued anyway. It can be seen through a variety of different cultures and periods in history that people have been trying to find a way to make love happen for a long time.

LOVE SPELLS IN POP CULTURE

From Tristan and Isolde to the 1970s television show Bewitched, love spells and magic have worked their way into our daily conversation. Through the powerful influence of plays, books, movies, music, and television series, both the image of the witch and our opinion of the magical arts have changed forever.

In a 12th century legend, an Irish Princess, Isolde, is on board a ship from Ireland to marry King Marke of Cornwall. She is escorted by Tristan, the King's loyalist and nephew. Isolde, having already fallen in love with Tristan, compels him to take poison with her – that they die together instead of her marrying King Marke. However, her maid, Brangane, prepares a love potion instead of poison, making the two fall passionately in love with each other.

The 1959 Clovers song, *Love Potion No. 9*, tells of a man consulting a gypsy for a love potion that worked a little too well. The song remained so popular over the years that it was later transformed into a movie with Sandra Bullock. After taking the potion, it makes people of the opposite sex become completely infatuated with them simply by the sound of their voice. Then you have the hit song, *I Put a Spell on You*, made famous first in 1956 by Jay Hawkins and later re-recorded by Nina Simone (my favorite version.) Of course, who can forget the song's inclusion in the 1993 film *Hocus Pocus* starring Bette Midler?

There are three episodes of *Bewitched* I can recall that focus on the love spell. In the episode "Make Love Not Hate," a love potion meant for Esmeralda ends up in the clam dip at the Stephens' party. In "Once in a Vial," after Samantha rejects an old boyfriend named Rollo, he tries to use a love potion on her that Endora accidentally drinks. In the episode "The Generation Zap," Endora hexes the daughter of Darrin's client so that she has the hots for him. So, you can see this theme was prevalent in television of the time. In the *I Dream of Jeannie* episode, "There Goes the Bride," Jeannie puts a love spell on Tony, which displeases Haji, the Master of all Genies. Haji makes Tony have several accidents that can only be undone if the love spell is taken off him.

Movie scripts have a long-term relationship with love spells. One of my favorites is the 1958 film *Bell, Book, and Candle* starring Jimmy Stewart and Kim Novak. Adapted from a 1950 play, a witch bored with her life casts a love spell on her neighbor. Many of the characters show how much Sol Saks, the creator of Bewitched, was influenced by this movie. In the 1998 movie *Practical Magic*, a spell is cast to keep love away. Young Sally casts a love spell so that she will never fall in love, asking for qualities in a man that couldn't possibly exist - "He can flip pancakes in the air. He'll be marvelously kind. And his favorite shape will be a star. And he'll have one green eye and one blue." Of course, later in the movie, the man with one green and one blue eye arrives and has all the other qualities and abilities she mentioned. But this is an excellent example of a love spell that requests certain attributes but doesn't cast upon a specific person.

Wood engraving by Charles Jameson Grant, ca. 1833.

Another example is the 1987 movie, *The Witches of Eastwick*, with Cher, Michele Pfeiffer, and Susan Sarandon. Their main characters gather together and begin harmlessly talking about the perfect man and what qualities they would like him to have, followed by Sarandon's character adding, "a foreign prince riding a great black horse." The next day, the Jack Nicholson character arrives in a black limousine. So here, you have a love spell that not only describes the perfect person for them but asks that he come to town. This is a wonderful way to construct a spell – detailing your desire then asking it to be put into action. The problem was that everything they asked for dealt with surface traits – that he be handsome, that you could talk to him, the size of his penis. They didn't ask that he be a nice person. So, the devil himself shows up. Be specific in your spell work.

Whether it was by watching *Charmed* or *Sabrina the Teenage Witch* or humming along to *Witchy Woman* by the Eagles, we've been inviting love spells and witchcraft into our homes and lives for decades. Now that spells have become "normal" to us, more people are turning to the magical arts to help shape their love lives.

MECHANICS OF LOVE MAGIC

ARE LOVE SPELLS ETHICAL?

The ethics of performing a love spell to attract someone against their will has been debated at great length. Some magical practitioners believe that if the person is not in a relationship with another, it is okay to cast a love spell on them. Others think that there is nothing wrong with casting a spell on someone as long as they are harming no one. But that is where the debate comes in. Many would say that as much as we may want to believe that the victims of our spells are not being harmed by them, that tampering with someone's free will, making them do what you want – not what they choose to do based on their own experience, could be considered a form of harm. Just because there is no physical harm involved –does not immediately give you the green light. Because manipulating a person into falling in love with another person (who they otherwise would not choose to fall for) is, to many people, the very heart of what makes it unethical.

SUBJECTIVE AND OBJECTIVE ETHICS

There are two kinds of ethics: subjective ethics and objective ethics. In short, subjective ethics is based on the idea that right and wrong decisions for one person may not be so for another; it is all due to an individual's circumstances, upbringing, and cultural background. Subjective ethics are dependent upon what someone feels is right or wrong based on their own opinion and how they would personally feel about performing magic if they found themselves in the other person's situation.

Ethics and cultural background can influence your magical path. For many Wiccans, casting a love spell on someone against their will is a major no-no because they subscribe to the three-fold law - whatever you put out comes back to you times three. But, for a practitioner of hoodoo, those rules do not apply. They would consider the spell to be more of a petition to God asking for this person's love. And if the spell does not work, God did not grant their request. This alleviates the spell caster from any backlash one way or the other.

ETHICS OF BREAKING UP RELATIONSHIPS

To perform a love spell that causes the breakup of an existing relationship is considered unethical by many people. Once you have the person you desire, how do you feel about someone else casting a spell to break the two of you up so that they can have your partner? It doesn't sound so appealing when the shoe is on the other foot. So, here you are – you have a lock of his hair, a back-to-back breakup candle, Breakup oil, a little graveyard dirt, and you're ready to start the work. You are going to get that woman out of the picture. He told you he loves you and wants to be with only you (but he's still living with her.) You put all your power into the work, and the candles burn well. A few weeks later, they start arguing. The following week, their relationship is history. He starts moving his stuff into your apartment. He is all yours now. Life is wonderful. So, another two weeks go by, and guess what? That ex of his? She just brought home a back-to-back breakup candle, some Breakup oil, and she's pulling his hair out of the brush he left behind. She's carving your name into one of the figures on the candle and his on the other. She's about to break the two of you up. So, tell me, why is she wrong for doing this? Why were you so right for doing it? He was with her to begin with – not you. It seems like she has every right, maybe more than you. This is where ethics comes into play.

But, there can be extenuating circumstances for breaking up a couple. For example, is one of them involved in drugs or criminal activity and dragging your friend down with them? Was he your love first, and she swept in and stole him away? If the two of you are meant to be together, and this gal got in the way, then it would be justified to separate them. What if you are married and your spouse is seeing someone else? Protecting your marriage most certainly warrants breaking the two of them up immediately. Magic and ethics are not always so black and white.

Should you break up a married couple so that you can have him? I find it amazing that so many people begin affairs with married men, break up the marriage, then are surprised when he later cheats on them. If your relationship starts with infidelity, there's a greater chance that it will eventually end that way too. It's true - everyone has the potential to slip up and make a mistake in their relationship. But if this married man has been seeing you for months or years, lying to and cheating on his wife the entire time, he is telling you something about his morals and ethics. What part are you playing in this game of ethics in your affair with the married man? So, you don't really have the right to act shocked if he cheats on you someday. I mean, he showed you in the beginning who he really was. You chose not to see it. If that is the predicament you find yourself in, I hate to tell you, but it is not all his fault. You picked the guy, knowing his ethics, and you looked the other way.

In short, ethics are associated with your character and how you conduct yourself – ethics are about morals, compassion, and what is considered right or wrong. Ethics can be influenced by religion (as well as many other factors). Your ethics decide where you draw the line between doing something that is considered unethical and making the conscious choice not to do it. But who decides what is and is not ethical? Ethics are based on an agreed set of societal terms about what is right and wrong and what is and isn't considered acceptable conduct. So, who decides? You do. Your neighbor, who also decides what is ethical in their world, may inform you that you are mistaken. And this is when conflict follows. I believe that every human has a built-in basic sense of what is "right" and "wrong." The problem is, we don't always listen to that inner voice when it conflicts with something or someone we have set our heart on. As a magical practitioner, I have witnessed that, where love is involved, people tend to throw ethics out the window.

MODERN LOVE ORACLE

There is plenty of fun and amusement to be had out of this novel article. You merely hold the "Oracle" in your hand, and placing it up to your lips, implant a kiss upon the two figures. Thenbreathe upon the palm of your hand, and place the Oracle upon the hand which you have just breathed on. Now is when the Oracle commences to do its "stuff." If the two figures rise up together, the person you are fond of LOVES you. If the figures remain stationary, the reverse is the case and you are "out of luck." The Oracle is also said to tell a person's character and disposition, whether you are going to marry, etc. For instance if the two figures on the Oracle kiss themselves, then it is a sign that you are in love. The Modern Love Oracle is about three inches in diameter, and takes up hardly any room in the pocket.
No. 3614. **The Modern Love Oracle** 15C
3 for 40 cents, or $1.35 per doz. postpaid

LOVE VS. LUST

To perform love magic, this is one of the first things you need to determine. Is it love, or is it lust? That goes for both of you. Is your relationship based only on sex? Is that the only reason he swings by your place? This can make the actual love work more difficult. But if there is even a spark of real emotions behind the sex, your spell just got easier.

Your approach to the work is essential too. I've seen many people (mainly women in these cases) spend all their time on magical work that is sexually based when what they are truly seeking is love. So, if you want this man to develop deep feelings for you, see you as his life partner, be the woman he takes home to meet his mother, stop using that penis candle as the puppet for all your spell work on him. Improving your sex life with lust spells is great, but you also need to work on his heart and mind if you want the relationship to last and have a deeper meaning.

E-pher Goddess amulet of sex, power, and fertility

It goes further than just love and lust, though. To construct the perfect love spell, you need to be able to look at and dissect the parts of a good relationship and be completely honest about what is not working, what may need to be repaired, or what may not be present at all. The elements of a long-lasting and healthy relationship are usually considered to be trust, communication, respect, acceptance, attraction, and love. If you stand back and look at your relationship in these terms, it will be easier to know where to focus your magic and, in turn, your real-world behavior. So, be honest about where you lack, so you know what to attack.

This may require a multi-part spell where you focus all your attention on each problem one at a time. I have often found that this type of work can be very effective – letting your spell work progress and build over some time by tackling it in very concentrated and detailed sections. After all, trust and attraction are two completely different energies, they have different motivations, and they *feel* different from each other. Better to perform them as two smaller spells; each one is fixating only on that issue. Mixing these two different energies into one spell would only weaken its efficiency, in my opinion. Remember, slow but steady wins the race!

Gemstone phallic symbols can be used in sexual magic

RECONCILATION AND REUNION

Reconciliation Spells are used to get an ex-lover to return, either permanently or just for a short time, depending on what you want. However, reconciliation magic is one of the most complex types of love magic, so it will take a lot of hard work and dedication to succeed. Why so hard? Because there are so many outside factors that people don't consider when planning their spell. So, you see them in the store with a basket full of red and pink candles, love oils, rose petals, a packet of lavender buds, and a little male voodoo doll – all ready to head home and light those candles then wait for him to walk back in the door. It is rarely that simple. Because this type of work addresses one problem – to bring him back. But, bring him back to what? To the exact same situation that led up to him leaving in the first place? This accomplishes nothing because he will most likely go again even if you do get him to return. For a return to me spell to be effective and long-lasting, you have got to ask the hard questions before your work begins.

- What caused the breakup?
- What part did I play in it, and have I corrected that problem or behavior?
- Is there any evidence they are working on their own bad behavior?
- Are either of you still angry?
- Are they already with someone else?

The answer to these questions is what can get in the way of your work. If you can correct them first, your success rate will skyrocket.

THE CUT-OFF POINT - SETTING DEADLINES

If you are working spells of reconciliation or trying to get a specific person to come to you, deadlines are an important component in your magic. Why? Because for your own happiness and sanity, there may come a point where you must admit they aren't ever coming back. I have seen people waste five to ten years of their life working spell after spell to bring back a specific person. Let me repeat that - five to ten years! When the truth is, they could have been in a fantastic, loving relationship that entire time if they had only let go and allowed someone better to show up. Deadlines should be based on reality without letting emotions override common sense. In other words, no deadline should be set that is unrealistic based on the circumstances. For example, if your significant other has been away for two years and you haven't heard from them since they left, a significant emotional gap has been allowed to set in. Getting them back could be more challenging than you think - sometimes, impossible.

When planning to work spells to bring someone back, timing is everything. How long have they been gone? Is it two days, two weeks, two months, or two years? The longer you let the time pass before working magic, the harder the task ahead. You have to strike while the irons are hot, so to speak. Start that spell when they walk out the door - not two years later when they are already in another relationship or, worse for your spell, married.

So, set a deadline, a cut-off point. Preferably one year or less. Six months is probably a better bet when you consider all the twists and turns our lives can take in that short time. They say it takes just six weeks to form a new habit. Get in there and get that love spell going before their new habits no longer involve you!

Pining for someone for years, someone who has clearly stated they do not want to be with you, is, at the very least, unhealthy - both mentally and physically. Once a deadline is set, you have to stick with it. If they love you and want to come back, then the spell should work. But time must be given a chance to do its thing before the deadline is up. For example, if your deadline was six weeks from now for them to come back into your life and they haven't shown any signs of being ready by week five or six - don't start casting again! You will end up messing everything up by sending the universe too many signals. I call this 'muddy magic,' - when someone keeps throwing magic against the wall to see what sticks. First of all, you are telling the universe that you have zero faith in any of the previous work you performed. Secondly, you have sent out umpteen prayers or intentions out into the world who, at this point, has no idea what you really want. Do it right the first time and wait it out. When the deadline passes; it is done and over with, so do not try again. They are either going to respond by showing up soon or not at all.

You can also use deadlines in spellwork that are aimed at a particular outcome rather than reconciliation. For example, if you make the deadline six weeks from now for your ex to return your phone calls, then I suggest that you stop calling them altogether. They are telling you loud and clear that they do not wish to speak to you. So many clients have said to me, "he's just stubborn, that's all." He has told you he does not love you. He has told you he is in love with someone else. He has told you he is never coming back. He won't return your phone calls. He has blocked you on social media. His family has stepped in and told you to leave him alone. In some cases, he has a restraining order against you. No, he is not stubborn; you are. Why aren't you listening?

Advertisements from the 1920s all the way up to the 1970s were
dominated by the man's misogynistic viewpoint of morality,
what women wanted, and what they were entitled to
– as demonstrated on the next few pages.

PREPARING FOR TRUE LOVE

The most effective love spells seem to be the ones that ask for the right love to find you – not the spells that try to influence a specific person. Because what it does is casts a broader net, if you will. The possibilities go from just one to the millions. It tells the Universe that you are finally ready to receive that one great love you have been waiting for all your life.

But, I can tell you that many clients I've seen do not want to entertain that kind of spell. They want that one guy and only him – the same guy that has been ignoring them for two years and is in a relationship with someone else. I explain that making room for a great love is like buying a refrigerator. You have saved up your money for the model you have been wanting. You make a trip to the store and finalize the sale, and arrange for delivery. But what happens when the delivery guy arrives? You never got rid of your old refrigerator. You did not make room for the good one, the right one, to show up. So, Mr. Right has to turn around and leave until you decide to get your act together.

THE IMPORTANCE OF SELF-LOVE

Learning to love yourself first is nurturing the most important relationship you will ever have in your life. Self-love not only boosts our mental wellbeing but creates more positive thoughts, reduces depression, and reduces stress. When you genuinely love yourself, you become the best version of yourself, which makes room for the *right* partner to come into your life if you are looking for love. And apart from mental wellness, loving yourself also provides you good physical health and boosts your immune system.

There is no denying that self-love is the essential ingredient for happiness. But first of all, it is important to understand its meaning. Self-Love means appreciating yourself as an individual, accepting yourself entirely without any expectation or judgment based on outer appearance and circumstances, financial stability, education level, etc. Loving yourself means accepting every part of your body – your height, weight, hair color, eye color, etc., even if it differs from what is considered "normal" or popular. It means being comfortable with who you truly are – regardless of what others think about you. For love to be true, it must be unconditional, without judgment. The same is true of self-love. Comparing ourselves to others is a waste of time. You are uniquely you. Please explain to me how you were put on this Earth to be someone else. I'll wait…..

The best example I've ever seen regarding self-love and self-worth is from the Julie Roberts movie *Runaway Bride.* Her character, Maggie, goes from relationship to relationship, leaving the guy at the altar each time because, basically, she has no idea who she is. She takes on each guy's likes and hobbies, down to what type of eggs he likes to eat. His favorite eggs become her favorite eggs. The first guy preferred scrambled; the next guy, fried; the next guy, poached. When Richard Gere's character calls her on her shit for not having a mind of her own, Maggie takes some serious time on her own to discover who she really is. Part of this was spending a day cooking eggs in every way possible and tasting them all. Eggs Benedict was the winner. And with this knowledge and a newfound sense of self, she is finally ready to make a true love commitment.

Magically speaking, what happens when we have taken the time to learn who we are as an individual? It raises our vibration to attract the love that is right for us. If you can't make decisions for yourself and feel you have no right to an opinion, then when you perform a love spell, you will attract the type of person who will think for you and tell you what to do. But, in taking the time to learn who you are, how to communicate your own opinions, and being confident in your right to speak your mind – you have just changed the love magic game. This version of you will not tolerate a lover that pushes you around. Loving yourself provides you with major upgrades when you start looking for a loving partner. In a nutshell, before you cast a love spell on someone else, ask yourself one simple question – what kind of eggs do I like?

THE LOVE ALTAR

Many love spell techniques typically involve prayer, visualization and other ceremonial practices. One of the most ritualistic love rituals is the construction of a love altar because its presence and use anchor our intentions and emotions towards creating and maintaining loving emotions or attracting new love to you.

A love altar, also known as a love shrine, can be created in any location: it can be placed on a bookshelf, in your closet or even at work. It is not necessary for the love altar to be anything fancy; there are many that have been created from a simple hanging shelf, a fireplace mantle, or even a wooden box that you keep closed and private when not in use. If you are already in a relationship, the altar should include items that are important to both partners and can be something as simple as a framed picture of you two together, or it could be an elaborate shrine with various symbols of love engraved on it. By including things that are of interest to both of you, you are creating a magical bond.

The first step in creating your love altar is deciding what kind of symbolism you would like to place on it. Symbols that represent love are often very simple and easy to find like hearts and roses. You might include pink, red, or white candles which can be simple votives or figural candles molded in the shapes of people. Use stones and crystals that represent love such as rose quartz for true love, lapis for good communication, and garnet for passion. Write down the lyrics to a love song that represents what you are feeling or wanting. It could be framed or folded then tied with ribbon as one of your ritual items. If there are any gifts the two of you have given each other, like a necklace, include that as well. It might be something as simple as the ticket stub from a movie the two of you saw together. Or, if you want to go the elaborate route, you might include as your centerpiece a statue of Aphrodite, the Goddess of Love (she was Venus to the Romans.)

Love Letters or love notes. It's true - not many people write love letters these days. But, has your love been texting you sweet (or sexy) messages? If so, print those out to include on your altar. After printing, anoint the four corners and the very center (this is called a quincunx or 5-spot pattern) with rose or lavender oil then fold the paper towards you several times. If you have a bottle of magical oil for love, even better. Other paper items you might include on the altar are cards you have given each other, a love poem you like, or even a sample of your love's handwriting.

But what if you are still looking for that one true love? It doesn't matter. You merely have to focus your energy towards attracting the mate that is right for you. Another type of altar might be about celebrating or strengthening an existing relationship. Place magnets or lodestones on the altar to draw new love to you. Write a love letter to your future partner and fix it the same way as the one we mentioned above.

By using your altar for ritual prayer or spells focused on love, it will raise your vibration to receive that energy when you go out public. But, do not forget the most important thing - in order to find that right one, you have to place yourself in situations to meet people. Accept invites to parties. Go with your friends to dinner. Say "yes" when they ask you to go dancing with them at the club. You never know when or where you might meet someone. Unless your true love is the pizza delivery guy, you probably don't want to spend all of your time in front of your altar - no matter how romantic and gorgeous you've designed it. Take all that loving energy you've been conjuring up and share it with the world.

LOVE POTIONS & NOTIONS

Casting love spells may require a few ingredients so that you can create your oils, powders, baths, and elixirs. Throughout the ages, love potions have been used for different purposes – to help married couples stay together, to solidify a good match in order to secure the family money, and even for winning cases in court. A potion (from Latin potio *drink*) is a liquid "that contains medicine, poison, or something that is supposed to have magic powers." We are going to explore all the ways to use magical ingredients for love including: on the body, around the home, by way of clothing, as oils or powders to anoint magical candles, and finally through food or drink.

For as long as love has existed, there have been love potions in one form or another. Love potions were sold at medieval fairs throughout Europe. These potions often contained ingredients such as ginger, parsley root, and cinnamon bark while others were infused with love-inducing scents such as rose and lavender.

One love potion that was said to be so powerful it required the consent of both parties involved in lovemaking called for a mixture of one pound each of chopped valerian root, gum arabic and sugar. This love potion is said to have made men more amorous, faithful, and honest when consumed with their favorite wines or dishes.

WEIRD HISTORICAL POTION INGREDIENTS

When we think of love potions, we picture a corked bottle containing a mystical brew of romance. But history tells us that the ingredients used were not all that appealing and sometimes illegal. Fresh blood, powdered bones, crushed insects - none of this sounds all that romantic by today's standards where we give bouquets of flowers and boxes of chocolates to entice love. All of these examples are presented for historical purposes. Their inclusion here is not a recommendation.

Sweaty Love Cakes - the Medieval Love Cake took elaborate steps to make someone fall in love with you. After mixing all the traditional ingredients for the cake (more bread-like as we would consider it today), the dough would be rubbed all over the naked body, including the genitals and armpits, to absorb the body sweat into the dough. It was then baked and fed to the object of their desire.

Spanish Fly - most people have heard of ' Spanish fly' mentioned in movies, television shows, and books. Also known as the Blister Beetle, it was used in potions dating back to Hippocrates. Latin writers document how the beetles were dried and crushed into a powder and then used as a potent aphrodisiac in numerous potions. These potions were said to be quite popular in the court of the Roman Emperor Augustus. Not recommended since Spanish Fly is considered toxic, causing permanent liver and kidney damage.

Bird Nest Soup - it is also known as the Caviar of

the East. Popular in China for over 1,000 years, it is used to stir up desire in the bedroom. Astoundingly expensive, it is made up of the saliva found on the nests of swiftlets. The nest is simmered slowly in water to extract the saliva, and the soup has a thin gelatin-like consistency.

Worms - for those wanting to explore the occult in the 16th century, many turned to the book *The Boke of Secretes of Albertus Magnus of the Vertues of Herbes, Stones and Certaine Beastes.* One formula for increasing the affections between a husband and wife was to crush earthworms and blend them with periwinkle, which was then mixed into a spouse's food.

In 17th century Mexico, women would crush worms to mix with herbs, milk, and corn to feed their man to keep him in love and at home. An alternative would be to rub it on his chest at night while they slept.

Murder - while parts of animals were often used in potions, so were human remains - even though many considered it taboo. A few harmless ways were by using a string of hair or menstrual blood as an ingredient. One especially dark recipe included the bone marrow and spleen of a murdered boy (not at all recommended.) But it could get more ominous, such as collecting bones from the graveyard to grind into powder.

Cobra Blood - throughout history and across many cultures, snakes have played a part in magical practice. In Indonesia and Southeast Asia, the cobra's blood is thought to kickstart the libido and get the sexual juices flowing. To drink the blood directly from the body of a freshly beheaded cobra is considered to be the most powerful.

Rhino horn powder - since the horn of a rhino could also be a phallic symbol, it is said that erectile dysfunction can be cured by consuming the powdered horn of this great beast. Keep in mind, as rhinos are on the verge of extinction, poaching them is illegal.

Leafcutter ants - in South America, Leafcutter ants have been eaten as an aphrodisiac to enhance sexual desire since pre-Columbian times. They are a traditional wedding gift in the region. What few may realize is that only the queen ants are edible. The legs and wings are removed before they are toasted.

Hummingbirds - thought to be supernatural in many cultures. Even today, practitioners continue to break the law by collecting the bodies of these regal birds on the black market and turning them into love spells. The body is wrapped in the photograph of the two lovers then placed in a jar where it is covered in honey and cinnamon to keep the relationship sweet and spicy.

After writing and rereading this selection of unsavory ingredients, I am reminded of the line from the Meat Loaf song - "I would do anything for love. But I won't do that."

HERBS & CURIOS FOR LOVE

Adam & Eve root – Adam and Eve roots come from the roots of the Orchid plant. The 'male' roots are more elongated and are usually the older roots while the 'female' root is rounded in shape and come from younger roots. They are used in pairs for love work, specifically to make a relationship more committed and secure. For this reason, many people turn to Adam and Eve roots for strengthening a marriage.

Balm of Gilead – said to ease the pain of a broken heart and to comfort those in need. Since it is known for calming arguments, it is often used in magic dealing with reconciling two people, to bring peace to a troubled marriage, and to help make a couple's home peaceful again.

Bay Leaf – this well-known culinary herb was once used to crown Greek victors. Brings protection, success, and visions. Can magically be used as an alternative to petition paper, similar to the way some write on bark. Can be used as a jinx deterrent by placing in the four corners of your property, your house, or a room.

Blood root - a native plant to the Americas, bloodroot was used by Native Americans to create dye but also for love. Magically, it is a marriage protector and aids in promoting harmony with family members, especially in-laws and helps prevent people from interfering in your marriage. Sew inside the pillow cases of you and your spouse if you feel someone is trying to disrupt your marriage.

Buckeye – carried to bring you good luck, money, and has also been used by some in divination. In the hoodoo tradition is said to keep you in 'pocket money.' In the love department, it can be used as a charm for male potency, to protect your relationship, and to heat up the passion between two people.

Catnip – used in spells for beauty and happiness, Catnip is also used to capture the heart of another and make them yours. Used for attraction spells, it is meant to draw people to you and have them bask in the glow of your company.

Coffee bean - increases powers of persuasion. Often used to stimulate spells and potions to make results happen faster. Used as an ingredient in passion spells to increase male desire.

Damiana - known as the 'love herb' it is especially useful in lust magic. Used to increase passion and spark an old love interest. Strong herb for use in all forms of sexuality magic.

Deer's Tongue - used in opening up communication, which is good for strong relationships. Can be used in drawing a love interest towards you.

Dixie John - also known as *Low John* and *Southern John*. Dixie John is used for matters that involve family life and love. Utilized to enhance your sex life and as a breakup ingredient against those who threaten your marriage. Also known as Beth root, Red Trillium, and Wake Robin.

Honeysuckle - used to bind a love interest to you. When infused in oil, can be used to anoint the forehead to increase psychic vision. Placed around green candles with cinnamon and alfalfa to attract money.

Hydrangea - often used in love magic as a replacement for Queen Elizabeth Root. Widely known as an unhexing plant that can be worn on yourself or scattered around the house. Some burn the root to rid a property of a jinx or curse. Use during uncrossing spells to help put up an extra barrier between you and the person you are trying to break free from.

Jezebel root - Jezebel Root is any of five species of Louisiana Iris, including; Iris fulva, Iris hexagona, Iris brevicaulis Iris giganticaerulea, and Iris nelsonii. Originally used by prostitutes to get paying clients, it is more modernly used to get money out of a stingy man. Many exotic dancers carry it on them to increase their tips. Another name for it is *Painted Whore*.

Lavender - a flower of friendship and harmony. While lavender is often included in love spells, it also helps to strengthen the bonds of friendship. Used to assist with sleep and rest and is also helpful in centering the mind for scrying. Worn to attract a new man or as protection from a cruel spouse. Also used in healing mixtures, to help see spirits, and is a powerful ingredient in purification baths. In aromatherapy, lavender is used for relaxation and to calm the body and mind. It is associated with the third-eye chakra, and used to center the mind.

Lodestone - has been used as a powerful amulet and Good Luck charm. It supposed to attract power, favors, love, money, and gifts. Can help to attract and bring into your life the things you want. Also known as a grounding stone.

Lovage - used to make one more attractive and alluring to anyone who looks upon them. To make one ache for you, mix lovage with Queen Elizabeth root and High John and bathe in for 9 days straight or take the same ingredients to make a mojo bag for love. An oil infusion of lovage is good for anointing candles of attraction. Also associated with psychic dreaming and purification.

Magnolia leaves - increases love and loyalty and encourages fidelity by placing under your mattress or under the bed. Used to solidify your commitment to each other. Can also be used in a controlling manner, to keep a man from performing for no one else but his wife or partner.

Marigold (calendula, aka *pot marigold*) - marigolds can be added to a magical bath for attraction and confidence, helping you to win over the respect and admiration of everyone you meet. Also used to create a happy, warm, and sunny atmosphere in the home.

Patchouli - patchouli is often associated with love and passion and relationships. In aromatherapy it is considered an aphrodisiac. But it is also strong in doing money and prosperity work - often used in money drawing oils and products or sprinkled around (or on) green candles.

Queen Elizabeth root - also known as Orris root. Most often used to attract men and have them fall in love with the one who carries the root. Promotes popularity, success, and aids in communication.

Racoon Penis Bone - also known as a *love bone*, it was an old Southern custom, most often used in Hoodoo, for a man to give one to a woman to show his intentions of love to her. An alternative would be for the man to bury the bone beside or beneath her porch to convince her to love him. Can also be tied underneath a bed to heat up the passion between two people by amplifying sexual pleasure.

Rose - used to induce dreams of one's future love. The main ingredient used in love spells. For emotions and divinity. To build a long lasting relationship.

Tonka bean - associated with the planet Venus, carry a tonka bean with you to attract love and romance. Some choose to carry 3, 5, or 7 beans corresponding to how many days they wish to draw out their attraction spell by carrying that many beans in their pocket then placing them under the bed in the evening. (considered toxic to consume in the U.S., also be careful around pets if you plan to place them under the bed)

Verbena - used for drawing in new love and breaking jinxes and to break bad habits and addictions. Used in glamour spells and for bringing inner beauty to the surface. Verbena was wildly popular in the Victorian era as an ingredient in perfumes, which led to its association and connection to beauty.

Violet leaf - calms the nerves, draws prophetic dreams and visions, stimulates creativity, and promotes peace and tranquility. Violet leaf provides protection from all evil. Used for love and romance work and to heal a broken heart.

vintage illustration of wild violets

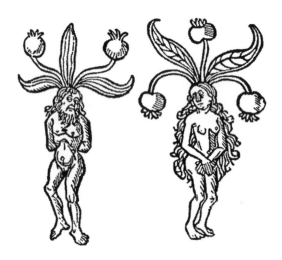

woodcarving of mandrake root as male and female

Spanish Fly

Leafcutter Ant

Buckeye

Tonka Bean

Hummingbird

Rhino Horns

Honeysuckle

Adam & Eve root

OILS FOR LOVE AND ROMANCE

There may be times when using essential oils are a better choice for creating your romantic concoctions. Many of the herbs previously mentioned can be found as an essential oil. But the oil may be easier to obtain in some cases. So, what is an essential oil? Essential oils, which are obtained through distillation or by mechanical pressing, are concentrated plant extracts that retain the natural scent and flavor of the plant. Other processes include expression or solvent extraction. They are used in perfumes, cosmetics, soaps, and other products, for flavoring food and drink (including candy and alcohol), and for adding scents to incense and household cleaning products.

Essential oils can come from many different sources, including herbs, flowers, trees, oil bearing seeds, and essential oil-bearing roots. Essential oils can vary within the same plant species, or from plant to plant. They may be inhaled, worn as a perfume, or incorporated into a carrier oil and are at the heart of what is known as aromatherapy. They are especially good for creating magical oils, baths, and powders.

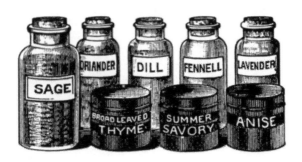

As a certified aromatherapist, I must encourage you not to ingest essential oils, no matter what contradictory information you read elsewhere. Over the years, I have witnessed many amateurs give aromatherapy advice in videos, articles, and during their home sales parties with no more training than what their sales rep's brochure provided. Some will tell you that only their brand is authentic because they have been taught to say so – mainly by the sales rep above them. I could go on and on about this subject but if you are truly interested, check out my book, *Essential Oils and Aromatherapy - How to Use Essential Oils for Beauty, Health, and Spirituality.* I use essential oils to scent (and imbue historical magic into) my anointing oils, sachet powders, bath salts, powdered incense, soaps, and massage oils.

Patchouli (Pogostemon cablin)

Amyris - calms the mind, eases irritability, promotes compassion. Also known as West Indian Sandalwood. Use in spells to get your partner to calm down and listen to what you're saying.

Basil – symbolizes happiness in the home, it can also be stimulating & energizing. Include in happy home spells to create a harmonious household.

Bergamot – uplifting and spreads happiness throughout the soul. Use after a breakup for heartache.

Black Pepper - an aphrodisiac, helps invigorate sexual energy. Being a pepper, avoid use in bath salts and massage oil. Increases psychic awareness so use in spells where you plan to plant thoughts in another, such as skull candle spells.

Cinnamon - attracts love, invigorates, and stimulates. Use to spice up your love life and ignite sexual passion. Used to draw a passionate lover to you. Trivia: the cinnamon in your kitchen cabinet is actually cassia.

Cedarwood – masculine energy. Helps to reduce stress, anxiety, and to disperse negativity. Use in spells to get rid of arguments and hostility.

Clary Sage - An aphrodisiac, brings on feelings of exhilaration. Used to sharpen the mind, good to use before elaborate rituals. Promotes vivid dreams, which can also be used to send dreams of you to your love target. Also good on skull candle spells to plant information.

Damiana - increases sexual arousal in both males and females, boosts stamina & increases orgasm. Use in spells of attraction and sex magick.

Geranium – said to increase fertility and draw in a new love. Often used to ease grief, breath in deeply and take a relaxing geranium bath after a bad breakup.

Goldenrod – a libido enhancer, goldenrod is also said to help remove emotional blocks. Good for blockbuster spell work.

Ginger - aphrodisiac that can increase sexual interest in a man. Heats up the bedroom. Tie a piece of ginger under the bed to spice up your sex life.

Jasmine – promotes true love and is considered an aphrodisiac. Sweet love, new love. Strengthens relationships or draws in a new one.

Juniper – use as a magical ingredient to heal the hurts in a damaged relationship.

Lavender – for long lasting love, helps promote monogamy. Calms volatile emotional states. Also used in same-sex love spells for attraction.

Lemon Balm – removes inner blockages, good for soul-searching and self-esteem.

Lemongrass – a good oil for lesbian love, it has long been associated with Goddess energy and feminine spirituality. Also increases feelings of inner peace.

Neroli - promotes self-love. Helps calm the mind for those worried about sexual performance issues. Helps create further emotional bonding during sex.

Orange – joy, inner peace, happy home life.

Peppermint – stimulating, can be used to clear the mind and see a situation for what it truly is.

Rosewood – used for attraction and stimulating passion, can also be used in spells for long-term relationships.

Vanilla – for increasing sexual arousal – especially in men. Associated with eroticism, it can add a sexual kick to your oil and bath formulas.

Sandalwood - Relaxes the nervous system to prepare for long sex sessions. Men wear sandalwood to attract a woman. Deep passion.

Ylang Ylang – used to attract and sexually excite the opposite sex. Mainly worn by women to attract a man. The flower petals are spread on the marital bed in Southeast Asia to ensure a night of passion.

PERSONAL CONCERNS

Personal concerns are elements that have either been a part of the body or have been worn on the body – a direct connection to the target of your magic. It can be blood, bodily fluids, hair, fingernails, and worn clothing. Used more in hoodoo than in witchcraft, you must be close enough to the person to obtain these personal objects.

Personal concerns might be considered a form of contagion magic. The law of contagion is a magical law that suggests that once two people or objects have been in contact a magical link persists between them unless or until a formal cleansing, consecration, exorcism, or other act of banishing breaks the non-material bond.

Blood – probably the most well-known and talked about personal concern is menstrual blood. In the hoodoo tradition, it is a common form of love magic for a woman to add a few drops of her menstrual blood to her man's morning coffee or place it in food that is served to him. In the South, it has become a common for mothers to warn their sons not to eat another woman's spaghetti early in their relationship, or he will become bound to her. The basis of this type of magic is the use of one's pheromones to lure in the object of their desire. It is known as giving a man "her nature."

Clothing – you want an article of clothing your target has worn but has not washed. This is because it still has elements of their sweat, dead skin cells, and possibly other bodily fluids. Underwear is the most popular article of clothing used in magic. Take a pair of his used underwear. Then get some twine and cut off a piece the length of his penis. This piece of twine is then anointed with your vaginal fluid. Cut another piece of twine large enough to go around your waist. Now tie the smaller piece of twine to the larger piece. Use the long piece to wrap around his underwear then tie it off. Either bury in the front yard or put in a jar and hide in a dark corner of your closet. You can also place ingredients like rose petals or lavender flowers inside the underwear and a photo of the two of you.

Foot tracks – the places where he has walked. If you cannot obtain personal concerns like hair or fluids, gather up the dirt where he has walked. A client once asked me for advice on how to do this. She really wanted to use personal concerns but had none of his. I asked her when he had last visited and she told me, "Two days ago." I asked her if it had rained since then – it had not. So, I had her sweep the porch from the steps to her front door, the natural path that someone would walk to come inside. She then used the collected dust as his personal concern, his foot tracks.

Hair – mentioned in almost all paths of folk magic, collecting a hair sample for magical purposes has made appearances in countless television shows and movies. The hair used can be from the head, the body, or pubic hair. There's an old piece of advice about never letting someone use your bathroom without first going in and cleaning out your hairbrush. As a symbol of perfect trust, Celtic men would sometimes weave a braid of their hair into a bracelet and gift it to the woman he loved. One suggestion is to go with him the next time he gets a haircut then "accidentally" drop your keys beside the barber chair and scoop up a little hair sample.

Handwriting – someone's signature or handwriting is an often-overlooked personal concern. A sample could be from a receipt, a document, the envelope from a birthday card (or the card itself.) A love letter would be best of all, but the practice seems to be dying out.

Nail clippings – you must already be on a domestic level with someone to collect their nail clippings. One way might be to mention they are too long for everything you want them to do to you during sex and offer to clip them for them.

Name papers – can't collect any bodily samples from a target? Use their name. Traditionally, one would write the person's name seven times on a piece of paper then anoint the paper with an appropriate oil. Fold towards you if you're asking for someone (or something) to come to you; fold away from you if you're wanting someone to leave. Some choose to burn the paper and use the ashes as the personal concern.

Photographs – you can often print out pictures of your target by going to their social media. For love work, it is a bonus if you have a picture of the two of you together. If you do not and need one for the specific spell you are performing, take a picture of each of you and tape it together. Want to use the photo of a couple to help break them up? Tear the picture in half and burn both pieces in two fire-safe vessels (like an ashtray or a cauldron.) If the object of your desire is one of those people, bury their ashes by your front door or in a potted plant in your house. Take the other person's ashes and drive them to the other side of town and dump out onto railroad tracks.

Saliva – saliva (or spit) can be used in the same way as blood, semen, sweat, or vaginal fluids. Magically speaking, possessing the DNA of another person gives you power and control over them.

Semen – considered the seed of life, magic with semen can be a powerful force. Women wanting to use a man's semen for magical purposes may collect it from a left behind condom, from the bed sheets, or sometimes through oral sex with the intention of keeping the specimen for later use. Two examples are to use it to anoint candles or rubbed on a doll that represents him. Men can use their own semen to anoint a photo of their love and place it in their left shoe in order to get them to come to him. If he adds his semen to his lover's perfume, no other man will want them. Anoint a piece of jewelry with semen then gift it to your lover to bind them to you.

Sweat – probably one of the easier personal concerns

to collect. Always keep a handkerchief on you. The next time a really hot day comes around, take it out and lovingly wipe your lover's brow with it. Use it to wrap magical objects you intend to use in your spellwork or use the fabric for a mojo bag.

Urine – historically, used by men in the same way that women have magically used their menstrual blood on their man. It can also have magical cleansing effects. If a sexual hex has been placed on you, pee into a body of running water while praying for release. Urine is the main ingredient found in witch bottles, which were used to counteract the powers of witchcraft by adding it and other ingredients to a bottle and burying it on your property.

cherub peeing in fountain statue

Vaginal fluid – used in the same way as menstrual blood. A well-known method is for a woman to take a figure candle in the shape of a penis and masturbate with it to later burn as a part of their spell. Their target's name, birthdate, and any other pertinent information can be carved into the candle.

Despite these historical rituals, I'd like you to consider *not* using bodily fluids. There are more health risks to deal with in our modern world than when these traditions were formed. For example, the old rootworker of the 1930s did not have to worry about HIV when they dispensed magical advice to clients about collecting personal concerns and feeding them to another.

Examples of diseases spread through blood or other body fluids:

- Hepatitis B - blood, saliva, semen, and vaginal fluids.
- Hepatitis C - blood.
- Human Immunodeficiency Virus (HIV) infection - blood, semen and vaginal fluids, breastmilk.
- Cytomegalovirus (CMV) infection - saliva, semen and vaginal fluids, urine, etc.

In my opinion, there is no need to feed another bodily fluid to weave your magic when there are plenty of other methods that will achieve the same thing. If you insist on using them, consider restricting their use to things like adding to your honey jars, anointing petition papers, and rubbing on candles. Beyond that, there are still the safer choices such as hair, fingernails and toenails, handwriting, and photographs. Ultimately, the decision is yours. But I felt it important to share with you my views on how to safely use personal concerns in the 21st century.

LOVE TOOLS & SUPPLIES

CANDLES

Candles are probably the most widely-used tool in spellcasting because they are easy to use but effective. Everyone who has blown out birthday candles while making a wish has performed the basic elements of casting a spell.

1. Decide on your goal
2. Imagine already achieving that goal
3. Put your intention into action and focus your will on its manifestation.

The size of the candle you use is not the most important thing. A larger candle can help you with a prolonged ritual that lasts several days or, if your goal is simple, a smaller candle that burns in two hours might suffice.

CANDLE COLORS:

White – Purity, blessing a relationship or marriage

Pink – For the deep, emotional aspects of love

Red – to signify the passionate side of love

Orange – road opening, bring in new opportunities

Yellow – for happiness in the home

Green – for financial problems that strain a relationship

Blue – healing physically and emotionally

Purple – success in whatever your spell commands

Black – absorb negativity that is damaging a relationship

CANDLE TYPES:

Figural – molded in the shape of people or objects. In love magic, the single man or single woman candle is used to signify an individual you want to target. There are hugging couple candles for strengthening a relationship. Then, there are conjoined candles with a man and a woman: front-to-front (facing each other) is for bringing two people together; back-to-back is for breaking two people up. For sexual magic, there are candles in both the shapes of the penis and the vulva.

7-day – intended to be burned over a period of seven days, these are candles encased in glass. Prayers or petitions are placed beneath the candle.

Chime – small tapers you will find in about every new age shop in existence. They are most often referred to as spell candles but are also marketed as chime candles because they are also used to generate a spinning movement with certain metal chimes. Burns over a period of around two hours.

Offertory – straight candles a little larger than the small chime candles so expect a longer burn time. Great for spells and rituals that require longer time to work, and the candle has enough surface for you to carve your intentions onto the surface. They are sometimes called household candles because they are the same size as the candle used for power outages.

Pillar – comes in a variety of heights and widths, pillars are usually thick, free-standing candles with plenty of surface for carving words, names, and sigils. Sometimes found as *drop-in* candles specifically meant for carving where they are then dropped down into a glass vessel for burning.

Votive – A votive candle or prayer candle is intended to be burnt as a votive offering in an act of Christian prayer, especially within the Anglican, Lutheran, and Roman Catholic Christian denominations. Can be used for short prayer or spell work. Burns around ten hours and needs a glass votive holder to keep them intact.

Tealight – typically burns between three and five hours, these are short candles usually contained in a thin metal cup.

Candles that are poured directly into glass or containers can be blessed and dressed by carving names or initials into the top of them then anointed with oils and herbs. Go sparingly. Too much oil will drown the wick and cause the candle not to burn. I usually touch my index finger to an open bottle of anointing oil then rub it on the top of the candle. A little is all you need. Just a sprinkle of herbs - too many will catch fire and interfere with how the candle burns.

Candles that are not encased like figural candles, chimes, pillars, etc., can be carved into. The carving doesn't need to be deep. Scratching names, birthdates, zodiac signs, sigils, and prayers is enough to impart your intentions. When anointing free-standing candles, rub the oils upward (from bottom to top) to bring something to you; rub oils top to bottom to get energy away from you.

The type of candle you use for your work is a personal preference and is sometimes chosen according to how long you want the spell to last. Cross candles can be used to represent a person when you don't have male of female candles around. Genitalia candles can be used to either spice up your sex life or to bind someone, sexually, to only you.

DOLLS AND POPPETS

In folk magic and witchcraft, a poppet is a doll made to represent a person, cast spells on that person, or aid that person through magic. In hoodoo, they are known as *doll babies*. What about the term *voodoo doll*? Although the use of the term *Voodoo* implies that the practice has links to either the religion of Haitian Vodou or Louisiana Voodoo, it does not have a prominent place in either. Rather, the term was made popular by the movie industry. The poppet's origins are in British witchcraft. Each culture that adopted it gave it their own style and variations on the ways to use it.

The way you care for your doll completely depends on the purpose it is intended. Just as each situation would be handled differently in a real-world way, the same applies to caring for a poppet to affect those real-world situations/problems magically. You can anoint your doll with an appropriate oil for your case to baptize it for that person. Some people choose a color that coincides with what they are trying to achieve.

Love doll - this type of doll baby should be cuddled and kissed on. Whisper to it all the things you want your lover to know. Tell it how it feels about *you* as well. Sleep with the doll for the first three nights, just as you would a mojo bag. You can either continue to sleep with the doll baby after that or tuck it into its own space each night with a goodnight kiss.

Passion doll -cared for in the same way as a love doll, a passion doll goes a few steps further. It is best to make this doll a little smaller so that it fits in your underwear comfortably. Kiss this doll, talk sweetly to it, rub it sensually all over your body each evening. Sleep in underwear at night so that you can tuck the doll away against your genitals. Since this doll will be so close to sensitive parts of the body, go easy on or avoid anointing oils that may irritate the skin. Craft the doll from a soft material.

Baneful doll - when using a doll baby for baneful work, like hot-footing an enemy or trying to control their actions, you treat the doll the opposite way you would a love doll. Scream at the doll, tell it that it is unwanted, that it must do as you say. Do not sleep with a baneful doll baby. Each night, wrap it in a dark cloth and put it in the darkness of a closet. Some use pins in baneful dolls, but your harsh words and dominating speeches can play the most important part in the work. When you no longer wish to continue this type of work with the doll, you can either burn it and throw its ashes off your property (at a crossroads is best) or throw it in a running river.

OTHER FORMS OF DOLLS AND EFFIGIES

Some of the best magic is set out in plain sight for everyone to see. If keeping a poppet or doll is too risky for you, there are several things that can be used in their place that can represent a loving couple. When I was a child, my mother had a pair of porcelain figurines of two angels kissing. This would be the perfect thing to anoint in marriage and love oils and could easily be left out in the open. Another example is something called Magnetic Dogs, which have been sold as a novelty for years. It is a pair of Scotty dogs (Scottish Terriers), one black and one white, which face each other kissing and, as their name implies, are magnetic – perfect for filling the shoes of any spell that calls for lodestones. Even a pair of male and female Madame Alexander dolls would work. A set of Raggedy Ann and Andy dolls could easily be filled with herbs, pictures, roots, and stones then sewn back up. So, if you cannot keep a traditional *voodoo doll* hidden, there are several options available to you. Use your imagination.

LOVE CHARMS

ATTRACTING LOVE WITH CHARMS

Charms are used mainly for bringing good luck or good fortune to you, which is why you hear the term 'lucky charm'. The word comes from the French word charme (pronounced *shom*), which initially meant spell or incantation. These charms were words that were used to bring about change, whether spoken or sung. An example of a spoken charm from Britain is to yell "bad harvest, bad harvest!" when the crops were growing well so that the Gods wouldn't grow jealous of man's good fortune and destroy them.

So, historically, charms weren't always tangible objects that you carried or wore - they were spells that you spoke to bring about what you wanted. Today when we say *charm* most people think of charm bracelets without realizing that those dangling gold and silver bobbles have a magical history. Others have no interest in or don't believe in such things. But it is interesting how those same people have a lucky tie they wear to job interviews or a lucky fishing cap. Or maybe their grandmother's ring makes them feel protected when they leave the house. I know I feel better if I am wear my saint medallions necklace.

There are many charms associated with love from all across the globe, and throughout most of history they held magical meanings. During the early 20th century, Queen Victoria inspired the elite class of Europe to wear charm bracelets. The Queen not only loved to wear them herself, but she also loved to give personalized charm bracelets as gifts to others. When her husband Prince Albert passed away, the Queen had a *mourning* charm bracelet made with a locket of the prince's hair and tokens of their life together.

Charms went from being symbols of spirituality and superstition to pieces of fashionable jewelry, and people throughout Europe could not get enough of them. Charms bracelets and necklaces were worn as lockets, glass beads, and family crest, as the wealthier class wanted to show off their fortune by wearing exotic clothing and fashion accessories.

The symbols themselves can be used to bring love to you just by wearing them close to your skin or can be magically enchanted by anointing them with oils. A charm does its charming through the power of its symbol and what that symbol stands for, such as the heart.

But what if you could turn a simple charm into a powerful talisman of love that would draw love to you? Before we get into how to do that, it is crucial to explain the difference between a charm, an amulet, and a talisman.

holy medals can be used as both charms and amulets

CHARMS, AMULETS, OR TALISMANS?

We covered what a charm is, but how is an amulet different? Amulets are primarily used for protection and to prevent unwanted energies from reaching you like harm, illness, or hexes. We're talking about objects that you wear or carry with you to protect you magically -- not physically. A good example comes from the Sheila Paine book *Amulets: Sacred Charms of Power and Protection*. She explains that a chunk of meteorite worn to protect against gunfire is an amulet, but - a bulletproof vest is not.

Today, some people may think of and use particular charms *as* amulets, and when an amulet is mentioned, we still tend to think of a piece of jewelry like a brooch or a necklace. But the earliest ancient amulets came from nature in the form of roots, nuts, beans, and things like animal bones and teeth. In our shop, aromaG's Botanica, we carry water buffalo teeth which is considered to be a symbol of masculinity and virility. So, if you've been having a problem in the romance department, you might carry one with you in the daytime then slide it under your mattress at night for safekeeping. While people have worn a shark's teeth for centuries, it is a modern custom for swimmers, fishermen, and surfers to wear a necklace with a shark tooth on it to protect them against drowning or other problems out at sea.

That is the thing about amulets - for the most part, they simply *are* magical by nature - you do not have to do anything to them to make them that way. In hoodoo, we know that the High John the Conquer root is magical on its own for commanding power, to gain personal mastery, and to make sure you are never at a loss for money. High Johns are considered to be masculine in energy. On the feminine side, we have the Queen Elizabeth root, which is primarily associated with women for good luck in love affairs, romance, marriage, and matters of passion - often to draw a man towards them. Pyrite is another good example. It is used to bring in money, increase business, and for good luck in gambling. So, while you could easily turn any of these three into a piece of jewelry or carry them in a mojo bag, there is no pressing need to. They are magical in their own right.

Now we move on to talismans. They are usually made for a specific person. Historically, it was crafted using a particular metal or gemstone to tie it to its owner, such as a birthstone. Sigils, prayers, Runes, Hieroglyphics, or seals of Solomon might be painted or carved onto the piece. The Native Americans would use teeth, bones, or furs from powerful animals like the bear because they believed it gave them the bear's power. We see this in some Hoodoo products that include the hair of a black cat, where it taps into the mystical energies.

Here is where a Talisman is different from an amulet: 1. It is crafted to *be* magical. It is designed that way, usually for a certain purpose. 2. A Talisman draws in power or enhances the power of its owner. While an amulet deflects ill intentions, a talisman can absorb positive energy towards it. The definitions may be different depending on your path. Nordic traditions think of the terms as synonyms because of their linguistic roots. But, if you research further, you will find that they think of a talisman as something engineered to be magical.

An easy way to remember the difference between an amulet and a talisman is alphabetical. An amulet (the letter **A**) is for keeping bad things *away* from you. A Talisman (the letter **T**) is for bringing things *towards* you.

ACTIVATING YOUR LOVE TALISMAN

Now we will talk about how to activate your talisman - how to take it from an everyday charm and turn it into a magical one. One of the most important things to do is to pray over it. I would do this over a certain period of days. Many people choose seven days straight, repeating the same prayers into the object. You can hold it while doing this, but I would not wear it yet - not until you have completed your ritual. Some people choose to light a candle beside it for each day of their prayer.

In our book, *Amulets, Charms, and Talismans in the Hoodoo and Conjure Tradition*, my co-author, Catherine Yronwode, mentions enchanting jewelry by placing it beneath an overturned plate then burning a candle each day for seven days on top of the plate. After that, you would take the jewelry and wear it against your skin. Talk to it, touch it often, and sleep with it for another seven days.

It is a Wiccan tradition to place the amulet or charm in the center of a table and surround it on four sides with things representing the four elements of earth, air, fire, and water. If this method appeals to you, four things that you could use would be a small dish of dirt to signify earth, a burning stick of incense for air, a candle for fire, and a glass of water for – you guessed it, water. If I were to do this, I would probably choose spring water or rainwater versus water from the tap since it might be more in tune with nature.

You might want to anoint the object with a special dressing oil created for the same purpose you want your talisman to stand for – love for love, passion for passion, etc. If you do not want to use oil because it may ruin your charm, you can always use sachet powders. If it can be immersed in liquid (such as a stone), you might choose to soak it in an herbal bath or fixed bath salts. This is why you often find hoodoo products in three different ways: oils, powders, and salts. While each one is used for the same purpose, they don't fit every situation. In this case, you decide based on instinct or what material your charm or amulet is made of.

If the amulet you are creating is of a love or passion nature, it is not uncommon to dress the object with your sexual fluids or the sexual fluid of your partner - or both. You can create an entire ritual around it by laying it on a bed of rose petals and surrounding it with pink candles. The best day to do this would be Friday because of its association with Venus and love. Choose pink candles for deep emotional love and red ones for the passionate side of a relationship. Or a combination of both. Don't forget to anoint your candles with a condition oil that deals with love, passion, or attraction, depending on your intention.

Some people find more simplistic approaches that do

not have a lot of ritual in them. They merely state their intention and what the talisman should be used for, then feed it with something like perfume or whiskey. Others smoke or smudge it the same way you would cleanse or bless an object. However, in this instance, you are using the smoke to infuse the charm with your prayers.

You can use any of these as a guideline to create your ceremony. Or, consider borrowing elements from two or three rituals to make a new and unique method. But one of the most critical elements is to use every bit of your undivided attention and energy while performing it - focus on what you want this talisman to stand for.

CHOOSING A CHARM

You know what you want to achieve, you've figured out what type of ceremony would be right for you, and now it is time to pick out just the right charm. Choose something that has meaning to you, one you can connect with. It could even be a piece of jewelry you already own. Some people like to choose a symbol from their heritage, such as the Irish Claddagh ring or something they find familiar like a four-leaf clover. There are hundreds of possible choices, so don't be afraid to take a little time to find the one that is right for you. I decided to showcase eight possible charms for love, sex, or fertility.

Four-leaf clover keychain

Luckenbooth - the Luckenbooth brooch is a traditional Scottish love token: often given as a betrothal or wedding brooch.

Claddagh - a traditional Irish ring that represents love, loyalty, and friendship

Heart Locket – a symbol of love or loving friendship that opens to reveal a compartment for objects, usually space for two small pictures.

Third Pentacle of Venus - a Solomon seal that is said to attract love when shown to anyone. It bears, among others, the Name of Angel Monachiel.

Dove - a symbol of love and peace. Doves appear in the symbolism of Judaism, Christianity, Islam, and Paganism.

Engagement ring – can be anointed with magic to help in strengthening a marriage or bring back a lost spouse.

Sheela Na Gig - figurative carvings of naked women displaying an exaggerated vulva. Used for fertility, sexuality, and sometimes protection.

Palad Khik - is a kind of Thai amulet shaped like a penis. The phrase "palad khik" means "honorable surrogate penis." A phallic representation of Shiva, it is also considered an animistic symbol of fertility.

This is just a small sampling. To research over 150 charms and amulets, check out our book, *Amulets, Charms, and Talismans in the Hoodoo and Conjure Tradition* by Catherine Yronwode and Gregory Lee White.

Scottish Luckenbooth

Irish Claddagh

Heart Locket

Third Pentacle of Venus

Dove

Engagement Ring

Sheela Na Gig

Palad khik

THE LOVE SPELLS

Here I have collected over fifty-five spells that deal with love, reconciliation, attraction, marriage, lust, fertility, and even how to break up a couple. They come from various sources from all over the globe – some dating back to as far as the 1400s, others very modern, and some originals were written by me. In some cases, I took a very old spell and reworked it for the 21st century. You will also find a few from my fellow spellcasters who were kind enough to contribute their knowledge in casting love spells.

The best advice I could give about casting spells is to have patience. They are usually not an overnight fix, although I have seen some proceed rather quickly. Spells are about manipulating the energy around us so that situations, people, motives, and emotions will take a turn in our favor. Patience includes the day you cast the spell. If you are pressed for time – postpone the work. I have seen people chant two sentences, light a candle, and walk away thinking they had accomplished something. Then they wonder why the spell did not work.

How badly do you want what you are asking for? Are you ready to do the work? Your spell should be given the same care as cooking a Thanksgiving dinner – not a frozen pizza. The more effort you put into your magical work, the greater your chance of success. After your spell is cast, monitor your behavior. Are you conducting yourself in a way that will lead you to your goal, or are you sabotaging yourself with your own actions? Only you can answer this.

ATTRACTION SPELLS

New Lover Needle Spell

Take two sewing needles and lay them side by side, pointing in opposite directions, head to point. Take a fresh leaf from a very tall tree and rub it down with rose oil. Another option is to use a fresh bay leaf. Dried bay leaves are too brittle to roll. Roll tightly around the two needles. When fully encased, begin wrapping the entire package with red thread from top to bottom, tightly, until it is several layers of thread deep. Place into a decorative pouch and sew shut. Traditionally, it was sewn into a leather pouch. Wear around your neck underneath clothing to attract a new lover. Anoint pouch with more rose oil whenever you feel it needs a little pick-me-up.

Bring the Right Love to You

You will need an undyed muslin or cotton bag - synthetic fabrics will not work. Brew a strong cup of tea using hibiscus flowers and rose petals. If you can only get hibiscus in a teabag, use three. If you have loose hibiscus, use a tablespoon of hibiscus and about a teaspoon of dried rose petals. When it has steeped for about 8 to 10 minutes, place the muslin bag down into the tea and leave it for at least half an hour – longer is better. When enough time has passed, pull out the bag and squeeze out excess liquid. Press between paper towels to pull out more moisture. You now have a pink bag. Allow to air-dry overnight. Take a pink piece of paper and cut out a square approximately 3 x 3 inches. Write out your name seven times on the paper. Now, turn the paper once clockwise. Write *the one for me* seven times across your name (with the words creating a hashtag). Now take a small pebble of rose quartz and place it in the center of the paper. Fold it towards you. Keep turning and folding towards you as many times as possible, then place in the dyed bag. Sleep with the bag in your pillowcase at night and carry it with you during the day.

Different Ways of Meeting Your Mate

Illustration from The Art of Kissing: a 1936 Guide for Lovers

Love Attracting Double Mojo

this mojo bag is to help the right love to find you. What you will need:

- Small square blue fabric (preferably silk, about 3 x 3 inches)
- Blue thread
- A snippet of your hair
- Love Attracting oil
- Lavender buds
- A coffee bean
- Red flannel square of fabric (about 5 x 5 inches)
- Twine or red thread

If you are feeling apprehension about cutting your hair, it does not have to be a long, noticeable strand. It can be snippets from the ends. Gather this hair in the center of the blue cloth and gather up into a little pouch. Begin to wind the blue thread around the neck of the cloth where it gathers together, making sure to wind facing towards you. When you have finished, tie off and anoint the bag with the love oil. Now take the square of red flannel and place in the middle of it: the coffee bean, a pinch of lavender buds, and the small blue mojo bag. Gather up just as you did the first bag and tie it off, once again winding towards you. Your blue bag containing your hair and the love oil should now be encased in the red flannel mojo with the other ingredients. Sleep with the double mojo bag for three nights in a row and carry with you whenever you go out in public. Is said to draw the attraction of true love.

Notice Me Fire and Ice Spell

This is for grabbing the attention of someone who just doesn't seem to notice you. Tapping into the energy of how opposites attract, it is intended to make them notice your good qualities that they are not seeing. You'll need a pink taper or offertory candle and a smaller yellow candle. Carve your name, dob, etc., into the pink candle and their name into the yellow candle. Light yellow and drip all over the pink candle. Get a large fire-safe bowl and a smaller fire-safe bowl that will fit inside the larger one. The pink candle goes in the smaller vessel. In the larger bowl, place nine ice cubes and the rose petals. Burn candle halfway down. Next night, pour off melted ice cubes and save the water. Repeat the spell with nine new ice cubes and more rose petals. Allow the candle to burn the rest of the way down. Take the melted ice water from both days and add it to your bathwater.

Rose Petal Spell

This is best performed on a full moon. You will need 3 vases, 6 roses, jasmine oil, and a bowl. Put two drops of jasmine oil in each vase and fill halfway with water. Put two stems of roses in each vase. Pick a petal from each vase one at a time, going back and forth between vases as many times as needed. With the pulling of each petal, say out loud a characteristic your true love should have. Drop in the bowl. When finished, take petals to a public park and drop them around the base of the oldest tree you can find. The wind will carry the rose petals to your true love and bring them to you.

Attraction Ritual

This Attraction Ritual is both a spell and a divination all in one! You will need the following:

- Bowl of Water
- Red (Sexual Relationship) or Pink Candle (Romantic Relationship)
- Incense
- Two Matches
- Love Drawing Oil

Directions: First, prepare the candle by etching both your name and the name of the one you desire in its wax. Next, dress the candle with your chosen condition oil. The condition oil you choose can vary depending upon 1) your sexual orientation (i.e. Lavender Love Drops for a Gay relationship, Come to Me for a Straight relationship) or 2) the type of relationship you desire (i.e. romantic or sexual).

Light the candle and incense. Then light your first match saying "this is me". Allow the match to burn for a few seconds then drop it in the water. Next, light the second match and say "this is (name of person you desire)". Again, let it burn for a few seconds and then drop it in the water.

Now dip your finger in the water and run it around

the rim of the bowl several times as you make your prayer of petition. You have several choices including:

- An extemporaneous prayer
- An Affirmative Prayer
- An affirmation or mantra (For example, "John loves Mary. John loves Mary. John loves Mary.")
- A Bible Verse (Psalm 23, Song of Solomon 8:6, Colossians 3:14, 1 John 3:18) Please note you may have to re-work the verse to fit your need.

When you are done, contemplate the bowl of water and watch the matches. If the matches come together, the person will be drawn to you; if they should separate, it indicates that your spell has failed and the one you desire is not likely to desire you in return. If the matches should come together and then cross one another forming a T, it means that the person you are interested in will come to you, but the relationship will not last.

Carolina Dean - www.carolinaconjure.com

Come to Me

Light a pink candle at sundown for five nights in a row. Anoint with Come to Me oil and allow to burn for 15 minutes. Say the name of the person you want to come to you three times in a row every night when you light the candle. On the sixth night, anoint a piece of frankincense and a piece of myrrh with the Come to Me oil, grind up the frankincense and myrrh tears, and mix with finely ground lavender buds and five-finger grass. Mix all together while saying your target's name. Light as an incense outside your door to draw them to you.

I Ache For You Spell

To make a man ache for your company and your kiss. Grind catnip, damiana, rose petals, bee pollen, and some menstrual blood. Mix well. Take a red male figure candle, and carve his name on it. Anoint the candle with love attract oil and dress the candle with blended herbs.

On a Friday night, create a sacred space in your bedroom and set the candle on your bedside table or altar. Before lighting it speak directly over the candle with your intentions (come to me, fall in love with me, be obsessed with me, etc.) When the candle is finished burning, wrap the wax in a red cloth and place it under the mattress until he comes to you.

- Miss Nikki Jean

Beckoning Gris-Gris

This is meant to act as a magnet to attract the right person for you. Usually not used on a specific person but to put the message out to the world that you want true love to find you. Get a pink or red drawstring bag and place inside: a piece of lodestone, lovage root, one nutmeg, and a pinch of rue. Rub a little Love Attracting oil around the inside rim of the bag before closing the bag. Sleep with the bag the first three nights then hang in a window that faces the street.

Condom tins from the 1930s

The Lovers tarot card from the Rider Waite tarot deck.

COMMUNICATION SPELLS

Make a Lover Communicate With Me

This spell is meant to open the lines of communication between you and your significant other. You will need:

- 2 pink figural candles (male/female, male/male, or female/female)
- 3 blue chime or offertory candles
- Communicate anointing oil
- Herbs - dandelion leaf, peppermint, yarrow flowers
- Optional - Chrysocolla Stone and blue string

Grind all herbs together. Anoint figural candles with oil and dress candles with herb mixture. Place figural candles on the tray facing each other. Now anoint three blue chime candles with the oil, and dress candles with herb mixture. Place candles on the tray in a triangle shape around figural candles. Spread any remaining herb mixture on the tray around all candles.

You can include Chrysocolla stones in your spell to increase calm and rational communication. Optionally, use a blue string and loop it over the two figural candles to link them together.

Pray your intentions onto the candles, letting the Universe know your communication needs. Light the candles and let them burn. Wrap any remaining wax in a blue cloth and keep it close to your lover.

- Reverend Roy - www.healingamulet.com

Honest Communication Spell

This spell is used when communication between you and your partner has become dishonest or hostile.

Write each of your names on two small slips of paper. Take a decorative, fire-safe bowl and place slips of paper in the bottom. Add a teaspoon of powdered sage on top of the name papers. Choose an attractive bowl that will go well with your decor, something you find appealing and looks like it belongs in the room. Fill 3/4 of the way up with sand. Add a teaspoon of salt and sugar and mix into the sand.

You will use this bowl as an incense burner. Put incense sticks standing straight up in the sand. Keep this incense bowl in the same room where you usually have conversations. The smoke from the incense signifies air and free-flowing communication. The sage in the bottom of the bowl will keep your words honest.

Optionally, you can place a few blue stones, such as lapis on top of the sand. Blue is the color of communication and the throat chakra.

Dream of Me

- Powdered incense for unhexing, such as St. Cyprian
- Fire-safe dish
- Red skull candle (or any red candle)
- 1 amethyst & 1 rose quartz
- Powdered clove & lavender buds
- Psychic Vision oil (or frankincense essential oil)

Light the incense in your fire-safe dish while thinking of the person who you want to dream of you. Carve their name onto the candle. Pass the candle through the incense smoke. This clears any blockages in your target's mind that may hinder you from penetrating their dreams.

Dress the candle with Psychic Vision oil, cloves, and lavender. These ingredients transmit what you want to project into your target's thoughts, control the narrative of their dreams, and allow them to experience their dreams peacefully.

Place the amethyst and rose quartz next to your candle (or, if they fit, embed them directly into the candle wax). The amethyst, a stone of psychic energy, amplifies the link between you and your target's mind. The rose quartz transmits loving, sweet feelings about you. Now, light the candle. While watching the flame, imagine the dreams you want to implant in your target's mind. Burn all the way through or for a few minutes a day over multiple days. Timing: It isn't necessary to do this spell while your target is sleeping.

- Virginia Tabor

I Call Upon Venus

This spell calls upon the goddess of love to help you spread the word that you are ready to rekindle an old love and get them to begin communicating with you again. What you will need:

- 4 new shiny dimes
- 3 pieces of rose quartz
- A scalloped shell
- 7 pomegranate seeds
- Square of white fabric
- Pink chime candle

Cut out a square of white fabric approximately 4 x 4 inches. Place on a solid surface. Set a small candle holder and your candle in the center of the material. Place the dimes heads up at the four corners of the square. Now place the three pieces of rose quartz on the straight sides of the fabric at north, east, and west. In the south position, place your scalloped shell and put the pomegranate seeds in the shell.

When lighting the candle, pray to Venus to send your voice out into the world to summon your lost love, asking them to begin communicating with you again. Alternately, if you are not calling upon a former love and want a fresh start, you might ask for the right love to find you. When the candle has finished, remove the candle holder and move the rose quartz to the center of the cloth. Set the dimes aside. If any pink wax has dripped onto the fabric, leave it there - don't throw it away. Put the pomegranate seeds in the center of the cloth with the rose quartz, then tie them up into a bundle. Keep the bundle in the vicinity of your phone (or where you charge your phone at night) and place the shell in your bedroom. Within at least three days of casting the spell, go out and spend the dimes in four different places so that they will circulate your message on their travels.

A scalloped shell is considered one of the symbols of Venus

Call Me Now Packet

This is to get someone to call you or get in touch with you in some way, such as text or email. Not only for love but this spell can also be used to get a potential new employer to call you. You will need:

- Yellow piece of paper
- Yellow chime candle
- Phone cord
- Dill
- Caraway seeds
- Envelope

Yellow is not only the color of happy times and good news; it also calls back to the days when the yellow pages were used often. If you can get a page from an old yellow pages book for your paper, even better. Light your yellow candle and keep it beside you as you work. It is a plus if you have any 'communicate' anointing oil. Use it to rub on your candle before lighting, rubbing the oil from the bottom to the top.

At the top of the paper, write the name of the person you want a phone call from, followed by your name on the following line. Repeat this pattern over and over until you reach the bottom of the page. Sprinkle a pinch of dill and the caraway seeds into the center of the paper. Fold the paper in three parts as if you were going to mail a letter. Now fold from left to right. Drop a few drops of melted yellow wax on the open end to prevent your herbs from escaping. Place in envelope and seal. Fold the entire envelope towards you twice. Now wrap the envelope with the phone cord. (you can usually find landline phone cords at $1 discount stores.) Leave envelope beside candle until it finishes burning. Set beside your phone at night while you sleep every night until you receive the call you've been waiting for.

SWEETENING SPELLS

How to Make a Honey Jar

Honey has long been considered to be a magical substance that can bring good luck, love, and prosperity into your life. The history of the honey jar can be traced back to African American folk magic and is mainly considered to be a tradition in hoodoo. When honey jars first became popular in hoodoo, they were mainly used for love to make the other person *sweet on them*, and the practitioner would choose a sweetening agent based on skin color. To sweeten a white person, corn syrup was used - if the target had brown skin, molasses was the favored choice. Plain sugar or sorghum were other choices. Honey was usually the last option because it was expensive and harder to obtain.

The point of a honey jar is to make your condition, and the people involved sweeter - more accepting, forgiving, tolerable, generous, or loving. It is considered to be slow and steady magic, not one that delivers fast results. But, don't discount the honey jar because of this. Magic that is slow-pouring and sticky like honey is better than immediate results that fade away as quickly as they are delivered. The jar can be as small or large as you prefer as long as you have enough sweetener to fill it. The jar must have a metal lid because you will be burning candles on top of it.

Always start by taking the time to thoroughly clean and dry your jar. I once witnessed in an online group someone sharing a picture of their honey jar with the Ragu spaghetti sauce label still intact! Of course, I couldn't scroll by without letting them know I doubted the results they'd get because of the lack of effort they put into creating the jar. Their response was, "Only the intention matters!" My point exactly. Their intention was to do the work quickly with no attention to detail, care, or pride in their spellwork. If you want results, don't be sloppy in your magic. Put in the effort if you want the work to pay off.

Once your jar is clean and dry, you may add a small number of herbs, roots, or flowers (or a mixture of them) that are magically associated with your situation. Write out your prayer or petition on a small piece of paper, fold it, and place it in the jar. Some prefer to use a picture of their loved one as their petition or a picture of the two of them together. Some write on the image. The choice is yours. Fill the jar with honey almost to the top, leaving a little room for possible (rarely happens) expansion. Say your prayer over the jar, dip your finger in the honey and taste it. Then screw on the lid.

Other items that can go in a honey jar:
- Personal concerns (hair, fingernails, etc.)
- Anointing oils
- Small charms
- Coins or medallions

Honey jars are not meant to be one-time spells.

Traditionally, jars are not reopened and tampered with once the lid is screwed on. They are continuously worked by lighting candles on top of the jar. You may dress your candles or leave them plain since your magical ingredients are already inside the jar. It is perfectly fine to use a candle holder, although some choose to warm the bottom of the candle and stick it in place in the center of the lid. When you first create your jar, light a candle every day on it for the first week or so. After that, you can back off to lighting a few times a week. Some workers light candles on their jars every day for months or even years to keep the work going and the energy building.

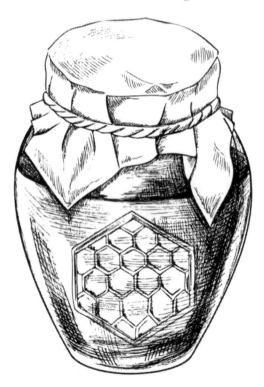

Five Cherry Spell

This spell falls between a passion spell and a sweetening spell because of its ingredients. It is meant to awaken your partner's desire in a way that they only have eyes for you. (Cherries stand for love, respect, fidelity, passion, honesty.) What you will need:

- 5 cherries
- Glass red wine
- Teaspoon honey
- Red bag or pouch

Pour the glass of wine, imagining that you are pouring it for your lover. Take a single sip of wine. Lick a small amount of honey from the teaspoon and eat a cherry. Take your time and make it a sensual experience as you roll the cherry around your mouth with your tongue while picturing you and your lover in bed. Take the remaining honey in the teaspoon and stir it into the wine. Spit the cherry pit into the wine. Repeat until you have eaten all the cherries and there are five pits in the glass. Allow the glass of wine with the pits in it to sit overnight. The next day, retrieve the pits from the wine and allow them to dry. You may throw away the remainder of the wine. Put three pits in the bag and place the bag under the center of your mattress. Put one pit in your underwear drawer and one in the bottom of his. If you fear he will find it, tape it to the bottom side of the drawer.

Mother-in-Law Syrup Jar

This is to get an in-law on your side and make them see and appreciate all your good qualities. Print out a small picture of something your mother-in-law enjoys, such as a hobby. It might be something as simple as a picture of a ball of yarn if she enjoys knitting. Write her name across the center of the paper, fold it towards you as many times as possible, and place it in the bottom of your jar. Add the following ingredients: balm of gilead and cloves for friendship, gravel root for favoritism, blessed thistle for her blessings, alfalfa for friendship, bloodroot for tranquility with family, and slippery elm so she won't gossip about you. If you know her favorite flower, add a few petals. Fill the jar with maple syrup and seal shut. Anoint a small yellow candle with your saliva and burn it on top of the jar. Repeat the candle burning three times a week, every week, for the first month. After that, burn a candle whenever you feel it is needed.

Sugar Bowl Spell

This spell gives the best results when you live with your target, *and* they use sugar in their coffee or tea. It is meant to make them act and talk sweeter and be more agreeable towards you. Write their name seven times on a small piece of paper and your name seven times in the other direction, creating a hashtag. Fold towards you several times and tape to the bottom of the sugar bowl. Fill up the bowl. Begin feeding your beloved the sugar in their tea, coffee, etc. If they do not use sugar in their drinks, use a pinch in their food daily – just a few granules.

Sweet Apple Spell

This natural sweetening spell doesn't require you to keep any part of it in the house with you. This may be important for some people whose partner knows they perform magic. Choose an apple that is known to be sweet, like Fuji, Gala, or Red Delicious. I am partial to Red Delicious both for eating and because they remind me of the apple in the Snow White story. You will need:

- 1 apple
- Honey
- Red yarn
- Personal concerns

Cut the apple in half. Spread honey on the insides of both halves. If you can get your lover's hair, place a strand on one side of the apple and a strand of yours on the other. If this isn't possible, carve your name into one half of the apple and your partner's name on the other. If you have that option, you may also use other personal concerns: fingernails, toenails, semen, vaginal fluid, etc. Put the two halves back together and begin winding the red yarn around the entire apple until it is held firmly back together. Bury in the yard. If that isn't possible, bury it in the bottom of a flowerpot. Their love will grow and sweeten on you as the days go by.

RETURN & RECONCILIATION SPELLS

Moving Candle Come to Me

this is to bring someone closer to you, perhaps someone you have an interest in, but the *spark* hasn't quite happened yet. This same work can be used for a spell of reconciliation. If that is the case, just replace the Come to Me oil with a Reconcile oil and write your petition accordingly. This spell calls for a male and a female figural candle. Replace, if needed, according to your sexual orientation.

- What you will need:
- 1 male figural candle, red or pink
- 1 female figural candle, red or pink
- Come to Me or Reconcile oil
- Rose petals
- 1 lodestone
- Paper and pencil
- Red or pink ribbon

First, carve the names for each person on the candle that represents them. For the male, write his name and on the female, her name. If you don't want to use a knife, you can easily carve words into the candle using the tip of an ink pen or even a toothpick. Rub the anointing oil into each candle over your carvings in an upward motion. If you happen to have hair from the person you want to attract, place it under their candle. You can do the same with your own.

These candles will melt and run across a surface. You need something flat with a lip around the edges to place the candles on. A cookie sheet lined with aluminum foil makes for a simple, easy to clean up workspace. Write your name on a piece of paper seven times. Now, turn the paper and write your love interest's name seven times so that it interlocks with your name. This will *weave* the two names together. Anoint each corner and the center of the paper with your magical oil. Place the petition paper in the center of the cookie sheet and set the lodestone on top of it.

Now, set each candle on opposite sides of the cookie sheet facing each other. It is not necessary to move them all the way to each edge. You want to leave enough room around the sheet so that you can sprinkle a ring of rose petals all the way around the two candles, locking them into a circle of roses.

Light each candle and state your intention. The wording doesn't have to be lengthy or rhyme. Simply speak from the heart and say what you want to happen. Some people choose to pray during this time. Every ten minutes scoot each candle a little closer to the center, about an inch or so. After doing this several times, the candles should be touching and on top of your petition paper. Now that they have moved across the surface and finally found each other, allow them to burn the rest of the way down without disturbing. The next day, gather the rose petals from the surface. You can either save them to use in a mojo bag later or sprinkle a few petals into your bath water on the days you plan to see your intended. Also, keep a little of your anointing oil behind your ears or on your wrists when you know the two of you will be together. Gather the foil around the wax and tie with a red or pink ribbon. Place under your bed for seven nights. After the seven days is up, bury in your front yard beside the porch to entice them to come to your house. If you live in an apartment, you can bury at the bottom of a potted plant. I knew someone who placed it in the bottom of the umbrella stand beside her front door.

Bed Broom Spell

This is an old hoodoo trick for bringing back a lover that has left. This is especially good for people who are married or have lived together. At sunrise, take two brooms. One represents you, the other for your spouse or lover. Put the brooms in the bed on the sides in which each of you slept. Now cross the brooms and pull the covers over the brooms. Leave there until nightfall.

Chicken Head Spell

An old southern spell from New Orleans to bring a husband back. Traditionally, the wife would take the head of a chicken and remove the main bone. She would then stuff nine pins or needles into the head then bury in the yard. When buried, she would write his name on a piece of paper and dress the paper with sugar, cinnamon, and white rum and nail it above the sill of the front door.

Cleanse Away the Trouble Between You

This spell calls upon the same energy as an unhexing or uncrossing spell by giving an effigy of the person a cleansing bath to remove whatever emotions keep you apart. What you will need:

- 1 Cross candle
- Hyssop herb
- 3 blue chime candles
- 3 pink chime candles
- 2 red chime candles
- Healing oil
- Love oil
- Small bowl

The cross candle represents your target. You can also use a male or female candle in its place if you wish. Carve your ex's name into the candle along with their date of birth. Secure the candle to the bottom of the bowl by slightly melting the wax underneath. Place the bowl on another fire-safe surface, such as a baking sheet. Pour about half an inch of water into the bowl and add about a teaspoon of hyssop to the water. Dip your fingers into the water and begin bathing the candle from top to bottom, careful not to get the wick wet. Do this several times while imagining their arguments for staying away are being removed. Think about what drove the two of you apart and try to only focus on what your ex had to say about it - all the things that, from their perspective, keep them from returning.

Next, dress the blue chime candle with your Healing oil. Dress the pink and red candles with the Love oil. On the baking sheet you placed the bowl upon, set the three blue candles in front for healing the relationship, the three pink ones behind the bowl to bring back the love, and a red one on either side to reignite the passion between you. Light all the candles, including the cross candle in the bowl. If anything is left when the candles have finished burning, you can bury it in the yard or dispose of it at a crossroads.

Plate Spell

This is another old hoodoo working for bringing back someone who has left. Write out your ex's name on a piece of paper three times across, all in one row. Write your own name below theirs. Set a plate on the table and put the paper underneath it. Sprinkle some sugar and raisins on the plate. You will call out the name of your beloved three times that day, each time lighting one of the candles. At nine in the morning, light the blue candle and call out their name, asking them to return. At three in the afternoon, do the same with the red candle. At six in the afternoon, light the white candle and call out their name again. Leave the plate there overnight. The following day, take the name paper from beneath the plate and pin it above the front door frame.

Face to Face Poppet Spell

It is a very English term, *poppet*. Whether you call them poppet or *voodoo doll* or, as in hoodoo, a *doll baby*, this spell teaches you how to take two of them and unite them in love. This can be for calling someone to you or for bringing back lost love. You will need:

- 1 red poppet
- 1 pink poppet
- Catnip
- Lavender
- Raspberry leaves
- Red thread

Take a pair of scissors and make a small incision in each poppet, just small enough to stuff in a few ingredients. First, name the poppets by writing out your name on a sliver of paper and place it inside one poppet and your lover's name in the other. Put equal amounts of the catnip, lavender, and raspberry leaves in each one. If you can obtain Adam and Eve root, place one in each poppet and sew back up. Now, lay them face to face and begin sewing around the edges, binding them together. When you have finished, hang it on the inside of your front door on the night of a full moon and leave there until the next full moon. Or, hang in a window that will allow the poppets to absorb the moonlight. If your love has not returned by the next full moon, put the poppet inside the pillowcase on the empty side of your bed.

Bring an Ex Back

This should be performed on the three nights of the waxing moon. Set a teacup facedown in the center of a piece of paper and trace a circle onto the paper. Remove the teacup; you will no longer need it. Take your time and use your best handwriting to begin writing your name and your ex's name side-by-side, over and over, all around the inside of the circle. Continue writing around the inside of the circle to create a spiral until you have reached the very center. Take a pair of scissors, cut out the circle, and add a dollop of honey in the center. Place four pieces of quartz crystal on the edge of the circle at north, south, east, and west. You will need three white candles; tealights are fine to use. On the same surface as the circle, light the first candle and allow it to burn all the way. Do the same with a new candle for the next two nights. When all the candles have burned, bury the four crystals at the four corners of your house. If you live in an apartment, leave inside and place at the four corners of the apartment - not in one room but the walls that make up your entire apartment. Take the circle and bury it in a flowerpot or below the mailbox.

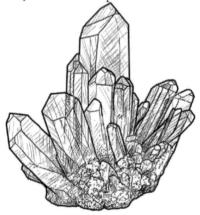

Mend a Breakup

This candle spell is meant to repair a breakup by recreating it then repairing the break.

- 1 pink chime candle
- 1 blue chime candle
- Reconcile oil

Take the pink candle and break it in half in the center but don't damage the wick. Anoint the entire candle with the reconcile oil. Light the blue candle. Hold the broken pieces of the pink back in place and begin dripping blue wax (the color of healing) onto the broken space. Continue dripping wax all over the pink candle, especially in the center, until you can no longer hold the blue candle safely.

Now place the pink candle in a candle holder and light. Concentrate on all the fun and loving moments of the relationship. Stay with the candle thinking these thoughts until it passes the point where the break was. From there, let the candle burn normally until it goes out.

PASSION & LUST SPELLS

A Woman's Mojo to Draw a Man for Sex

To make this little hand you will need the hair of the man you want. Pubic hair is best, but other hairs will do. Prepare a 3" square name paper by using red ink to write the man's name over and over in the form of a spiral leading to the center of the paper, where you will draw a heart. Touch the heart with your sexual fluids. Use menstrual blood if you have it available; if it is gooey enough, stick the man's hair right in it.

Fold the paper by the corners in method, and seal it with stick red wax or glue. Dress the paper with Follow Me Boy oil. Place it in a square of red flannel with a piece of Queen Elizabeth Root, two Red Rose Buds, two Lodestone Grits, Lavender Flowers, Spikenard, and other love curios, then sew the flannel into a packet small enough to wear on your person. Let your sweat get on it, then dress it with your own favourite perfume. If you wear it in your bosom, you will charm the man you desire with your special winning ways.

For female same-sex love, you may add Q Oil or Lavender Love Drops.

- Catherine Yronwode. reprinted with permission from her book, *Down-Home Sex Magic – Hoodoo Spells of Bodily Love*

Burning Desire Candle Ritual

Take a figural candle and carve your target's name into it. Then, carve words like sex, desire, passion, hot, sweaty, erection, orgasm, arousal, cum, and any other words you can think of that you would associate with hot, sweaty sex. If there were any words or phrases that mean something to you (or your target) during sex, use them. Now, slowly lick the candle from the bottom to the top as if your tongue were traveling over a lover's skin. Anoint the candle with your bodily fluids followed by Passion and Lust oil. Just like your tongue, anoint from bottom to top. This motion is said to bring things to you. To anoint a candle from top to bottom is for getting things away from you.

You will also need a second candle that will be used only for its flame. It can be any kind, any size, but it could also add to the power of your magic if you also anointed it with Passion and Lust oil. Light the second candle, and each night for seven nights pass the figural candle through its flame. Do not light the figural candle yet - merely pass it through the flame, back and forth, over the other candle. Do it quickly, not enough to melt it. The intention is to make the other person have a hot, scorching desire to be with you. On the seventh day, after passing it through the flame the last time, light the figural candle and allow it to burn. Magically speaking, it would not be unheard of to masturbate in front of the candle. You might receive a passionate visit or a lusty call even before reaching the seventh day of the ritual.

Aphrodite & Ares Hibiscus Tea
Materials:

- Empress tarot card (represents the goddess of love Aphrodite)
- Emperor tarot card (represents Aphrodite's lover, the god Ares)
- Dried hibiscus flowers
- Decorative container to store hibiscus
- Passion and Lust oil

1.) Place the hibiscus in the container.

2.) While holding both the Empress tarot card and Emperor tarot card, recite, "I call upon beautiful Aphrodite. I call upon fierce Ares. As they have an unquenchable thirst for one another, may they bring such passion and lust to me."

3.) Set both the cards down on top of each other. Place the container of hibiscus on top of the cards.

4.) Take a bit of the Passion and Lust oil and anoint the outside of the container (make sure not to touch any of the hibiscus). While anointing, recite, "O powerful Aphrodite and passionate Ares, I thank you for enchanting this hibiscus to bring passion and lust to me as quickly as you both conquered each other."

5.) Store the container on top of these tarot cards in a place they will be undisturbed for three days. You might choose to decorate this space with images of romance and sex. At the end of the three days, you may return the cards to your tarot deck.

Now the hibiscus is enchanted to bring you passion and lust. It can be used to brew up a daily drink (you're welcome to mix it with your regular tea mix). Or, you can use the hibiscus as components to other spells. You don't have to do this spell again until all the hibiscus has been used up.

- Virginia Tabor

Mars (Ares) and Venus (Aphrodite). Engraving by D. Marchetti

Cooking with Aphrodisiacs

You might consider cooking dinner for your intended after performing one of the love spells you found in this book because a great spell is planned out in multi-parts to increase its chances for success. For example, there is a Middle Eastern dessert called the Persian Love Cake that many believe inspires both love and lust. They say that if you slice the cake and eat it while looking at someone, they will become attracted to you. Of course, at least four of its ingredients are for romance - rose water, pistachios, ginger, and almonds. Here is a list of some of the top ingredients to use for increasing libido and getting in the mood for a night of love.

- almonds
- artichokes
- asparagus
- chocolate
- figs
- ginger
- oysters
- pistachios
- pomegranate
- spicy chili peppers
- strawberries

Using Penis and Vulva Candles in Spellwork

Lust and Passion spells are meant to ignite or awaken sexual desire. Some people use this to bring the spark back into an old relationship, while others want to increase someone's sexual desire towards them. Using candles shaped like the penis or the vulva is a way to connect directly with sex magic. True, they can also be used to kill another person's passion if that is your goal. But let's focus on spicing up your love life. You can, of course, carve names into them like you would other candle workings, but the physicality of how you interact with your candle can be even more potent. Spending time stroking the penis candle back and forth has a lot of power behind it, magically speaking. You can rub down the vulva candle with Passion and Lust oil and stimulate it with your fingers while thinking of your target. Both actions use friction to awaken sexual activity.

A woman may choose to masturbate with the penis candle before carving and anointing it for their spell. This act puts a lot of personal energy into it as well as their personal concerns. If a man works with a vulva candle, he might masturbate and ejaculate onto the vulva candle before beginning the magical work. If a couple is performing magic as a team, there are several creative ways they can use the candles with or on each other to imbue them with sexual excitement.

Tip: to avoid irritation, do not anoint your candles with any sort of condition oil or herbs ahead of time if you plan to use them sexually. Wait until afterward.
(see page 54 for illustrations)

101

Hot Sauce Floor Wash

This recipe makes a wash for your front porch that will attract a red-hot lover. Take a bottle of hot sauce and pour out about ¼ from the bottle to make room for more ingredients. Add to the bottle the following:

- 8 drops lavender oil
- 3 drops rose oil
- 6 whole peppercorns
- Pieces of orris root or hydrangea root
- 7 juniper berries
- Pinch damiana leaf
- Pinch of catnip

Shake well. Label the bottle so that you don't mistake it for regular hot sauce later. Take a half bucket of warm water, add a capful of the hot sauce mixture, and mop your front porch. Take your finger and rub a bit of the water on the door frame and across the threshold. If you live in an apartment, you may have to skip the mopping and simply anoint your doorway. Wash hands thoroughly afterward.

MARRIAGE & FIDELITY SPELLS

Dirt Dauber Spell

An old spell from Savannah, Georgia. Take an entire dirt dauber's nest (an abandoned one) and drop it into a full glass of water. Place a saucer on top of the glass. On the top of the saucer, place your lover's photograph. Let it sit for fifteen minutes. Take a drink of the water and from then on your lover will stay at home and by your side.

For Fidelity in a Marriage

After the wedding ceremony, set aside the bride's corsage and the groom's boutonniere. When the couple can be alone in private, dress the flowers with a tiny dab of Stay with Me condition oil and press them together in the family bible at the Songs of Solomon. If you are not of the Christian faith or are otherwise uncomfortable with the Holy Bible, you can use another book with meaning to the couple, such as a book of love poetry. Or, if perhaps you are both fans of the Lord of the Rings, you might want to use that book in place of the bible.

- Carolina Dean - www.carolinaconjure.com

Keep That Man At Home

Take one of his dirty socks, rub some of your bodily fluids on it, and tie a knot in the center of it. Place under mattress. An alternate method is to take one of his dirty shirts, put it against the mattress under the fitted sheet on your side of the bed, and sleep on it every night to keep him home. You can change it out with another unlaundered shirt, so he doesn't start wondering where his missing one is.

Repair a Marriage

This is for a couple that is still together, but things have either become stale, strained, or distant. The reason I mention that the couple should still be together is that this is a spell to strengthen and repair. If the couple were already separated, then a spell of reconciliation would be needed instead. What you will need:

- 1 white spell candle
- 1 pink spell candle
- Adam and Eve oil
- Two red 7-day candles
- Piece of thin wire, about 6 to 8 inches long
- 2 candle holders
- Picture of the two of you together

On the picture, front and back, write out all the things that attracted you to each other in the first place. You can mention things you like to do together, things in common, things that make you laugh, good memories – anything positive about the relationship. Be as detailed as you like. If you run out of space, write on top of the words you have already written. When you have finished writing, your mind should be in a happy place, thinking about all the great times and the high points of your union. Anoint the picture in the sign of the cross with the Adam and Eve oil with a dab at the top, bottom, left, and right. Add one more in the center of the picture then fold it towards you twice. Set out your candle holders and place the photo beneath them.

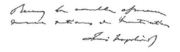

Next, choose one candle to represent you and the other for your spouse. Write your names on the candle that stands for each of you then anoint the candles with a little of the Adam and Eve oil, rubbing the oil with an upwards motion. Take one of the candles and place it in the candleholder. Now get your wire and curl one end around the candle. Place the other candle in the next holder and wrap the other end of the wire around the second candle. They should now be joined by the wire. Light the candles and allow them to burn until they are gone.

When they have finished, place the photo between the mattresses or tie to the bottom of the bed. Take the wire that bound the candles and wind it around the foot of the bedpost towards the head of the bed on the side your spouse sleeps. If possible, plan a night of romance in that same bed.

Romany Fidelity Spell

Take a red ribbon made of silk and cut it to the length of his erect penis. Keep the ribbon under your pillow. Seduce him into making love in a manner where you can collect some of his semen. Rub the semen on the ribbon, then tie it in seven knots. Secure the ribbon to the backside of the bed's headboard. Keeps him faithful to you.

Spell to Secure a Relationship

- Any Love Drawing oil
- Two lodestones
- Iron grit to feed lodestones
- Two red 7-day candles
- Rose, Damiana, Cinnamon, Honey
- Flameproof dish to perform the ritual
- A red flannel bag
- A small photo of you and your partner

This spell is powerful for attracting two lovers together and securing your love & marriage. Begin your work on a Friday, the day of Venus, at noon if possible. Burn Frankincense on a charcoal disk inside a flameproof container within the space. Fumigate the flameproof dish, the red flannel bag, the candles, your photos, and lodestones by burning a small pinch of the aforementioned herbs.

Now, write your name and birthdate on the backside of your photo, and the same for your lover. Very lightly anoint each corner and the center of both photos, on the front, with the Love oil. Place both photos on the flameproof dish on opposite sides. Now, take your 7-Day red candles, anointing each with the Love oil, dress each with a pinch of each herb, placing one 7-day candle on your photo, the other on your lover's photo. Dab a small amount of honey on each photo.

Now, take each lodestone, knock thrice upon both, one at a time, and speak, "Mighty lodestone, you who draw and attract, awaken now, and aid me to draw my beloved to me, ever with me, into my home and life, forevermore." Place a lodestone by your candle, the other near theirs. Sprinkle a pinch of lodestone grit on each, speaking, "As this iron grit is ever drawn, attracted, ever clinging and sticking to you, so my beloved and I are ever drawn, attracted, clinging to one another!" Dab a very small amount of honey onto each candle.

Burn a pinch of each herb, light each candle, and speak your desires to draw your love into your life and home, to sweeten your communication and your connection. Do this every day, for seven days or however long your candles may burn. Each day move both lodestones closer together and both of your candles and photos together. Each day, speak your desires, envision how it feels to be with your beloved, in love, and happy together. Sit with these emotions, let them fill you up as you see your heart's desire manifest!

Once your candles have burned down, place a small handful of the Rose, Damiana, and Cinnamon within the red flannel bag, along with both lodestones. Take your photos, place them face to face, and put them inside the red bag. Fumigate the bag with a final pinch of Rose, Damiana, and Cinnamon, and anoint with the love oil. To finish this work, conceal the red bag between your bed mattresses. Now the work is complete.

\- Adam Darkly of Devil's Conjure
devilsconjure.ecwid.com

Keep Him Faithful

When your lover is asleep, snip off a bit of their pubic hair. Cut a square of yellow fabric and place it in the center along with three coriander seeds and a pinch of marjoram. Hand-sew the edges all the way around with close stitches while concentrating or praying over their fidelity only to you. When you have sewn the square completely shut, thread a new needle and push the needle through the center of the bag you've made. Wrap the thread around the needle once and go back through the other side. Do this three times, then tie off the thread with three strong knots. Traditionally, one would throw this into a hog pen where it would be constantly trampled to *keep their man down*. In this modern world where hog pens are hard to come by, you can bury the bag in the yard near the front door.

Claddagh Spell

Print a nice picture of the Claddagh symbol, the appropriate size for a frame you've chosen ahead of time. Take a photo of the two of you as a couple and anoint with Marriage or Adam and Eve oil in the four corners. Allow to dry. Place your picture behind the picture of the Claddagh, frame, and hang where it can be seen every day to secure love, loyalty, and friendship in your marriage.

SPELLS OF FERTILITY

Pink and Blue Root Spell

You will need two Adam and Eve roots, male and female. (While they are the same root, an elongated one will represent the male, and a more rounded one the female.) Create a paste from flour and water, adding a few drops of rose water or rose essential oil. Use the paste to bind the two roots together. Take baby-blue thread and wrap around the roots to keep them together, then wrap again with pink thread (the traditional colors for male and female babies.) Place roots in a red flannel bag and put the bag under your pillow for the first three days. After three days, rub a little whiskey on the bag's outside, then place the bag under the mattress. Take back out once a week, dress with rose water and whiskey, and put back under the mattress.

Lucky Rabbit's Foot

A rabbit's foot is considered lucky throughout many cultures but is also a symbol of fertility. Pick out a rabbit's foot that calls to you and sleep with it in your underwear for seven nights in a row. Surround yourself with rabbit imagery such as pictures and figurines. Keep the rabbit's foot in your bedroom.

Ancestor Mojo

Create a yellow mojo bag and include violet leaves, raspberry leaves, grains of paradise, basil, magnetic sand, and a pinch of graveyard dirt from each of your deceased ancestors that you know would wish you well.

BREAKUP SPELLS

9-9-9 Spell

An old hoodoo spell to separate two people. Roll black candles in pepper and burn every evening at 9:00 pm for nine minutes for nine days. This could be brought up to date by anointing the candles in Breakup oil before rolling them in the pepper.

Backward Spell

To drive away the *other woman* (or *other man*) take their picture and write their name on the picture backward. Place the picture in a tealight candle holder face down. Take a tealight candle and anoint it with Confusion oil and Breakup oil. Drop the candle into the holder and burn. When finished, take the picture, put it in an envelope, and mail it to a random address in another state. Don't put a return address on the envelope.

Witchcraft Divorce Spell

You will need:

- 1 black chime candle
- 1 orange chime candle
- Rosemary oil
- Thyme oil

On a Saturday night, light the black candle and say, "Candle, I light you in the name of Hecate, to break up this married couple and make them divorce."

Take the orange candle and anoint it with rosemary oil. Say, "I consecrate this candle in the name of Juno, to bring divorce between these two people."

Put the candles side by side and let them burn down. To complete the spell to break up their relationship, you will then have to sprinkle thyme oil above a door where they both pass through.

Red Onion Spell

An old hoodoo spell where the onion symbolizes the tears you want to cause in a couple's household. Write the names of the couple you want to separate on a small piece of paper, with each name going up the page diagonally in different directions so that their names form an **X**.

Take a red onion and cut it down the middle twice so that it is in four even pieces. Put their name paper down in a jar along with the onion pieces. Heat some vinegar until it is warm, not hot, and pour into the jar. Seal and store in a dark place where it won't be disturbed or found. Take out and shake the jar whenever you want to ignite an argument between the couple.

Split Up a Married Couple

You will need a few chili peppers, oregano, a teaspoon of sulfur powder, dirt from a place where a fight or crime happened. Use about 6 cups water as a base and brew potion to a simmer, not boiling. _Do not drink_ - this is a steeping potion and not safe for consumption. Traditionally, one would also use dog feces and cat feces in this potion; that is up to you. You may want to cook this outside because of the pungent smell. You will need a wedding cake topper with a bride and groom. Drop the topper into the brew, cover with a lid, and leave there for three hours. After three hours have passed, fish out the topper and put it in a plastic bag. Dump the potion down the toilet. Take the topper to a bridge, remove it from the plastic bag and throw it off the bridge.

Back-to-Back Breakup Candle Spell

You will need:

- 1 Back-to-Back candle (black or red)
- Valerian root (crushed fine)
- Red pepper flakes
- 2 red chime candles
- 2 white chime candles
- 2 black chime candles
- Breakup oil
- Table salt

Breakup Spell to separate or break up two people using what is known as a back-to-back candle. It is the figure of a man and a woman positioned on the base of a heart, and they are facing away from each other. A candle where the lovers face each other would be used for a love or come to me scenario. Carve each side of the candle with the names of the people involved, their birthdates, zodiac signs, sigils, or anything else that would tie them to the candle.

Anoint both candles with Breakup oil and roll the candle in the crushed vandal root (valerian.) When it burns, this candle will form a puddle, so place it on a cookie sheet that you have covered in aluminum foil. Anoint all the chime candles with the Breakup oil and roll them in the valerian root. Place the back-to-back candle in the center of the cookie sheet, then slightly towards the front. Behind the main candle, position the two red chime candles. Place one of the white candles on either side of the red candles. Now, place one black candle on either side of the white candles. This signifies how their feelings towards each other will go from passion to bland to darkness.

Carefully draw a line of red pepper flakes from the front of the cookie sheet back to the chime candles in a way that it travels across the central candle at the feet of the couple. Now lay out a line of salt around the inside edge of the cookie sheet so that none of your work can escape. Light all candles and focus on the couple fighting, then no longer caring, then breaking up. When finished burning, gather up the aluminum foil. Dispose of it onto railroad tracks so that the couple will get far away from each other. (See front-to-front candle illustration on page 54, similar to what you will use.)

SPELLS OF CONTROL & INFLUENCE

Do As I Say

To command someone to follow your wishes. Write the name of your target seven times on a small piece of paper. Anoint the four corners and the center with Do As I Say oil. Fold paper towards you, turn and fold towards you again. Take a purple candle, light, and begin dripping the wax onto the paper until it is completely sealed on both sides. Carve your name into the wax on both sides, then seal by dripping more of the purple wax on both sides. Put into a purple fabric bag, tie off the drawstrings, then store somewhere high such as the top of a cabinet or pinned above a doorway.

High John Controlling Oil

Put High John the Conqueror root, rosemary, calamus root, and lodestone in olive oil in a small jar and place in a sunny windowsill for three days and three nights. Afterward, rub your hands with the oil when you intend to see the person you want to control, and make sure to touch their hands. You can also take a small amount and rub it on places you know they will touch - doorknobs, water faucets, toilet handle, a bar of soap in their bathroom.

Make a Lover Stop Wandering

This is a very traditional Hoodoo spell to make your wandering lover (or spouse) want to return home and stay there with you. Take their left shoe and anoint the bottom of the shoes with Return to Me oil, mainly towards the front of the shoe where the toes would be. Sift together equal parts of salt and pepper and drop them into the shoe. Stand at the front door and point the shoe inside (toes towards the inside of the house). Shake the salt and pepper inside the shoe as you walk towards the back door. Dump the contents out the back door. Salt and pepper the shoe two more times until you have performed this three times total, each time pointing into the house and shaking out the contents out the back door. When you have finished, place both shoes back where you found them but make sure to point them in the same direction as if the person were walking into the front door. Finally, dress the front door threshold with your Return to Me oil.

I Tower Over You

This is a simple, compelling spell to show your target you are the boss. You will need a white chime candle for your target and a larger, purple offertory candle to represent you. Anoint the white candle in Compelling or Control oil and wrap purple thread around the candle in single layers from top to bottom. Anoint the purple candle with your own saliva. Position the candles side by side and light. As you see, the larger purple candle looks down upon the white one, demanding its submission. In most cases, if you position the candles close enough together, the purple wax will spill onto the white, covering your target's candle with the power and sovereignty of your own.

Get Over a Love Gone Bad

For releasing the emotions you have for someone so that you can get past the pain and move forward. For cutting out the sting of a bad breakup or when someone never returned your feelings, it is time to cut things loose and clear the path for a bright future. Think of this as an influencing spell with yourself as the target.

- What you will need:
- 1 peony root
- 1 piece of Queen Elizabeth root
- Cut and Clear oil
- 1 black bag or square of fabric
- Black thread
- Photo of the person you want to get over
- 1 banana peel

Take a pen with black ink and cover the face in the picture with rows and rows of X's – all the way across the image, line after line, until the entire surface is covered. With each X made, you know that you are canceling your connection to this person. Take the piece of Queen Elizabeth root and place it under your tongue and say something to the effect of, "you no longer influence me. I cut away all emotional connection we had." Then, spit the piece of Queen Elizabeth root into the center of the picture. Fold the picture three times away from you.

Next, anoint the peony root with the Cut and Clear oil. Place the peony root on the center of the folded picture and fold it one more time, the opposite direction of your first folds (long ways) but still making sure to fold away from you, not towards. Take the black thread and begin winding it around the picture (moving away from you while wrapping) with both roots trapped inside until you have fully bound everything in a cage of black thread. Place into the black bag or tie into a square of black cloth. Wrap the banana peel tightly around the bag and bury it in the farthest corner of your yard. The peel will encourage worms to eat away at it, and as the bag deteriorates, so will your connection to this person.

Rose of Jericho Spell

The Rose of Jericho is used in magical work for its obvious connections to the concept of resurrection. In their native habitat, the plant turns brown and curls up when conditions are too dry. They then blow away and drift around like little tumbleweeds until they finally find a source of water. They appear dead but uncurl and spring back to life once they find water, earning them the name *resurrection plants*.

This spell takes several days of preparation because first, you will need to water your Rose of Jericho until it has reopened and turned green. Now take a piece of paper and write your name and the name of the person you want to control. Most use this for a *keep your man at home* type of spell. Your intentions will determine what kind of oil you anoint your name paper with. For this spell, we will assume you intend to prevent your love from straying, so rub a little I Dominate My Man or Controlling oil on the paper. Fold up the paper and place it in the center of the Jericho plant. Remove it from its water source and allow it to dry and close back up. When completely dry, place in a bag and tie under his side of the bed.

CONCLUSION

I began writing this book because how to perform magic for all matters of love is one of the most common questions we receive in our store. For that matter, love is the most requested type of spell work I perform for clients. It is the most asked-about topic when I perform tarot readings. Let's face it; love is on everyone's mind because we all seek it throughout our entire lives in one way or another. If you choose to perform any of the spells in this book, allow me to give you some final advice: cast them after carefully considering what is truly best for *you* in the long run – no one else. Emotions can take us to places we don't want to go and make us become people we don't care to be. Love yourself first.

BIBLIOGRAPHY

Wedeck, Harry E. *Love Potions Through the Ages – A Study of Amatory Devices and Mores.* Citadel Press. 1963.

Magnus Albertus, *The Book of Secrets of Albertus Magnus: Of the Virtues of Herbs, Stones and Certain Beasts.* R. Coats of London. 1650

Cunningham, Scott. *Magical Aromatherapy – The Power of Scent.* Llewellyn. 2006.

White, Gregory Lee. *Essential Oils and Aromatherapy - How to Use Essential Oils for Beauty, Health, and Spirituality.* White Willow Press. 2013.

White, Gregory Lee. *The Use of Magical Oils in Hoodoo, Prayer, and Spellwork.* White Willow Press. 2017.

Illes, Judika. *Encyclopedia of 5,000 Spells – The Ultimate Reference Book for the Magical Arts.* Harper Collins. 2008.

Bird, Stephanie Rose. *365 Days of Hoodoo – Daily Rootwork, Mojo and Conjuration.* Llewellyn Publications. 2018.

Wright, Elbee. *Book of Legendary Spells.* Marlar Publishing Co. 1968.

Yronwode, Catherine. *Down-Home Sex Magic -Hoodoo Spells of Bodily Love.* Lucky Mojo Curio Company Publishing. 2021

Yronwode, Catherine & White, Gregory Lee. *Amulets, Charms, and Talismans in the Hoodoo and Conjure Tradition.* Lucky Mojo Curio Company Publishing. 2021.

Hyatt, Harry Middleton. *Hoodoo, Conjuration, Witchcraft, and Rootwork, Volumes 1 - 5.* Memoirs of the Alma C. Hyatt Foundation. 1970-1978

Made in the USA
Monee, IL
01 August 2023

40240819R10070